4/14/10

ATLASES OF THE WORLD

ATLAS OF
AFRICA

RUSTY CAMPBELL, MALCOLM PORTER, and KEITH LYE

rosen publishing's
rosen
central

This edition published in 2010 by:

The Rosen Publishing Group, Inc.
29 East 21st Street
New York, NY 10010

Library of Congress Cataloging-in-Publication Data

Campbell, Rusty.
Atlas of Africa / Rusty Campbell, Malcolm Porter, and
  Keith Lye.
    p. cm. – (Atlases of the world)
Includes index.

ISBN 978-1-4358-8454-0 (library binding)
ISBN 978-1-4358-9111-1 (pbk.)
ISBN 978-1-4358-9117-3 (6-pack)

1. Africa–Maps. I. Porter, Malcolm. II. Lye, Keith.
  III. Rosen Central (Firm) IV. Title.

  G2445.C3 2010
  912.6–dc22

                                    2009582098

Manufactured in China

This edition published under license from
Cherrytree Books.

CPSIA Compliance Information: Batch #EW0102YA: For Further Information
contact Rosen Publishing, New York, New York at 1-800-237-9932

This illustrated atlas combines maps, pictures, flags, globes,
information panels, diagrams and charts to give an overview
of the whole continent and a closer look at each of its countries.

COUNTRY CLOSE-UPS

Each double-page spread has these
features:

Introduction The author introduces the
most important facts about the country
or region.

Globes A globe on which you can see the
country's position in the continent and the
world.

Flags Every country's flag is shown.

Information panels Every country has an
information panel that gives its area,
population and capital, and where
possible its currency, religions, languages,
main towns and government.

Pictures Important features of each
country are illustrated and captioned to
give a flavor of the country. You can
find out about physical features, famous
people, ordinary people, animals, plants,
places, products, and much more.

Maps Every country is shown on a
clear, accurate map. To get the most from
the maps it helps to know the symbols
that are shown in the key on the
opposite page.

Land You can see by the coloring on
the map where the land is forested,
frozen or desert.

Height Relief hill shading shows where
the mountain ranges are. Individual
mountains are marked by a triangle.

Direction All of the maps are drawn
with north at the top of the page.

Scale All of the maps are drawn to scale
so that you can find the distance
between places in miles or kilometers.

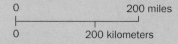

KEY TO MAPS

KENYA	Country name
～～～	Country border
■	More than 1 million people*
•	More than 500,000 people
•	Less than 500,000 people
☐	Country capital
ATLAS MTS	Mountain range
▲ Kilimanjaro 19,340ft (5,895m)	Mountain with its height

Population figures in all cases are estimates, based on the most recent censuses where available or a variety of other sources.

Nile	River
⊢⊢⊢	Canal
▬	Lake
⊢	Dam
⬭	Island

	Forest
	Crops
	Dry grassland
	Desert
	Tundra
	Polar

CONTINENT CLOSE-UPS

People and Beliefs Map of population densities; chart of percentage of population by country; chart of areas of countries; map of religions; chart of main religious groups.

Climate and Vegetation Map of vegetation from forests to deserts; maps of winter and summer temperatures; map of annual rainfall.

Ecology and Environment Map of environmental damage to land and sea; map of natural hazards and diseases; panel on endangered animals and plants.

Economy Map of agricultural and industrial products; chart of gross domestic product for individual countries; panel on per capita gross domestic products; map of sources of energy.

Politics and History Map showing pre-colonial events, slave trade routes and areas of recent conflicts; panel on great events; timeline of important dates; map of European colonies in 1913; flag of the Organization of African Unity.

CONTENTS

Chimpanzee
See page 17

AFRICA

Africa, the second largest continent, is changing quickly. Around 50 years ago, European nations ruled most of Africa. As countries became independent, the new governments changed the way they were ruled and new names appeared on the map of Africa.

Many countries adopted one-party governments. Others suffered civil war and came under military dictators. Above all, Africa faces a struggle against poverty and many of its countries are among the world's poorest. Farming is the main activity, but many farmers produce little more than they need to support their families. Mining is important, but most of Africa lacks industries.

Democracy has been hard-won in many African countries. Nelson Mandela was president of South Africa from 1994 to 1999. His 28 years in prison for his opposition to apartheid (a form of racial discrimination) in South Africa has made him an international symbol of liberty.

People South of the Sahara the continent is populated by black Africans, who speak more than 1,000 local languages. By contrast, in North Africa, the Arab and Berber people mostly speak Arabic. Disease and poverty are widespread and life expectancy is less than 50 years.

Spectacular sights attract an increasing number of tourists to Africa. The Victoria Falls, on the border between Zambia and Zimbabwe, is one of Africa's many scenic attractions. Local people call it Mosi-oa-tunya, or "the smoke that thunders."

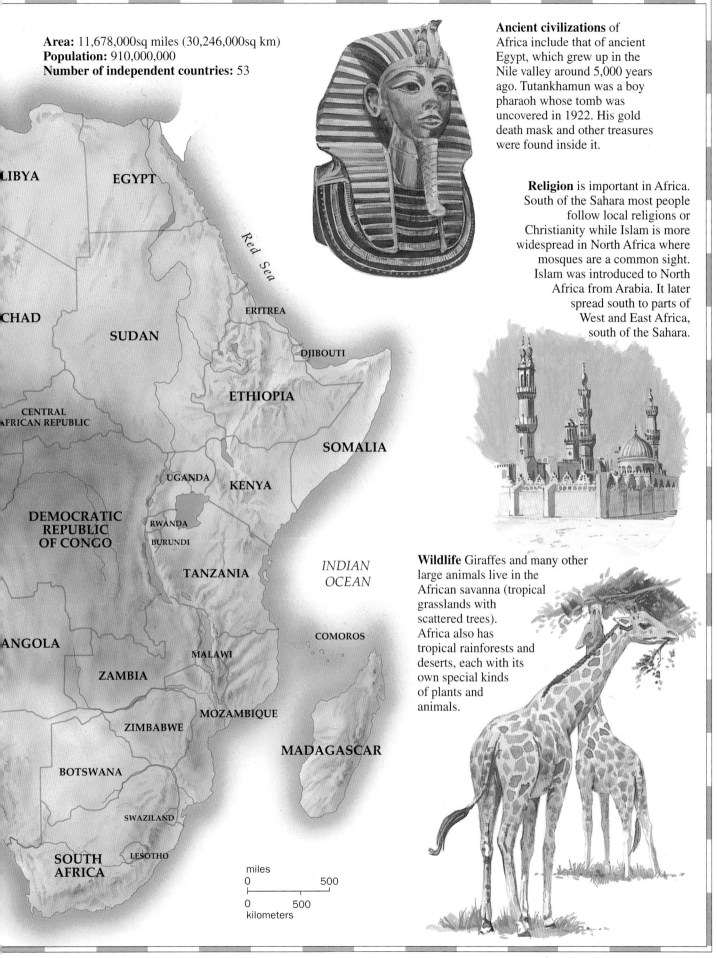

Area: 11,678,000sq miles (30,246,000sq km)
Population: 910,000,000
Number of independent countries: 53

LIBYA

EGYPT

CHAD

SUDAN

ERITREA

DJIBOUTI

CENTRAL
AFRICAN REPUBLIC

ETHIOPIA

SOMALIA

UGANDA

KENYA

DEMOCRATIC
REPUBLIC
OF CONGO

RWANDA

BURUNDI

TANZANIA

Red Sea

*INDIAN
OCEAN*

ANGOLA

COMOROS

MALAWI

ZAMBIA

MOZAMBIQUE

ZIMBABWE

MADAGASCAR

BOTSWANA

SWAZILAND

SOUTH
AFRICA

LESOTHO

miles

0   500

0   500
kilometers

Ancient civilizations of
Africa include that of ancient
Egypt, which grew up in the
Nile valley around 5,000 years
ago. Tutankhamun was a boy
pharaoh whose tomb was
uncovered in 1922. His gold
death mask and other treasures
were found inside it.

Religion is important in Africa.
South of the Sahara most people
follow local religions or
Christianity while Islam is more
widespread in North Africa where
mosques are a common sight.
Islam was introduced to North
Africa from Arabia. It later
spread south to parts of
West and East Africa,
south of the Sahara.

Wildlife Giraffes and many other
large animals live in the
African savanna (tropical
grasslands with
scattered trees).
Africa also has
tropical rainforests and
deserts, each with its
own special kinds
of plants and
animals.

NORTHWESTERN AFRICA

Northwestern Africa consists of three countries and one territory, called Western Sahara. Western Sahara was once ruled by Spain and called Spanish Sahara. It is now occupied by Morocco, but many of the local people have fought to make their country independent. The main regions of northwestern Africa are the fertile northern coasts, the high Atlas Mountains, which run through Morocco, Algeria and Tunisia, and the huge Sahara desert.

ALGERIA

Area: 919,595sq miles (2,381,741sq km)
Population: 32,930,000
Capital and largest city: Algiers
(pop 3,060,000)
Other large cities: Oran (638,000)
Constantine (443,000)
Official language: Arabic
Religion: Islam
Government: Republic
Currency: Algerian dinar

MOROCCO

Area: 172,414sq miles (446,550sq km)
Population: 33,241,000
Capital: Rabat (pop 1,759,000)
Other large cities: Casablanca (3,344,000)
Fez (904,000)
Marrakesh (872,000)
Official language: Arabic
Religion: Islam
Government: Monarchy
Currency: Moroccan dirham

TUNISIA

Area: 63,170sq miles (163,610sq km)
Population: 10,175,000
Capital and largest city: Tunis (pop 1,996,000)
Other large cities: Sfax (285,000)
Official language: Arabic
Religion: Islam
Government: Republic
Currency: Tunisian dinar

WESTERN SAHARA

Area: 102,703sq miles (266,000sq km)
Population: 273,000
Government: Status disputed, but occupied by Morocco.

Atlas Mountains These high ranges extend about 1,490 miles (2,400km) across Morocco, Algeria and northern Tunisia. The highest peak is Jebel Toubkal, in Morocco's High Atlas range.

Ceuta (Sp)
Tangier
Kenitra
Rabat · Fez
Casablanca · Meknès

MOROCCO

ATLANTIC OCEAN

Marrakesh · High Atlas · G R A N D
Toubkal
13,665ft (4,165m) · G

Agadir

CANARY ISLANDS (Spain)

Laâyoune

Western Sahara

Ad Dakhla

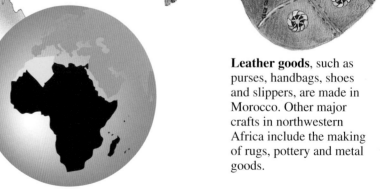

Leather goods, such as purses, handbags, shoes and slippers, are made in Morocco. Other major crafts in northwestern Africa include the making of rugs, pottery and metal goods.

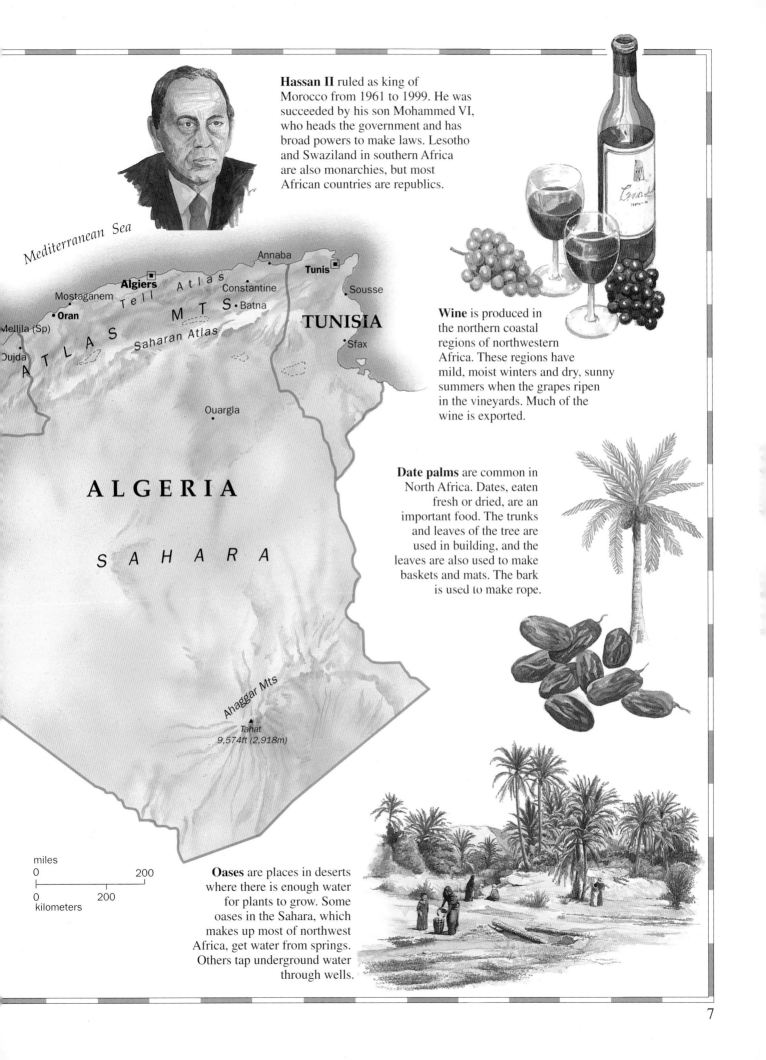

Hassan II ruled as king of Morocco from 1961 to 1999. He was succeeded by his son Mohammed VI, who heads the government and has broad powers to make laws. Lesotho and Swaziland in southern Africa are also monarchies, but most African countries are republics.

Mediterranean Sea

Annaba

Tunis

Algiers

Mostaganem

Constantine

Sousse

Tell   Atlas

Oran

M T S

Batna

Mellila (Sp)

Saharan Atlas

TUNISIA

Oujda

A T L A S

Sfax

Ouargla

A L G E R I A

S A H A R A

Ahaggar Mts

Tahat
9,574ft (2,918m)

Wine is produced in the northern coastal regions of northwestern Africa. These regions have mild, moist winters and dry, sunny summers when the grapes ripen in the vineyards. Much of the wine is exported.

Date palms are common in North Africa. Dates, eaten fresh or dried, are an important food. The trunks and leaves of the tree are used in building, and the leaves are also used to make baskets and mats. The bark is used to make rope.

miles
0   200

0   200
kilometers

Oases are places in deserts where there is enough water for plants to grow. Some oases in the Sahara, which makes up most of northwest Africa, get water from springs. Others tap underground water through wells.

Northeastern Africa

The Nile valley was the home of Ancient Egypt, one of the world's earliest civilizations. Like its oil-rich neighbor Libya, it became part of the Roman Empire. Other ancient kingdoms developed in Sudan, Africa's largest country. Egypt has many factories, but farming is the main activity of the people in Sudan. The main religion of the region is Islam. In southern Sudan, where black Africans follow local religions or Christianity, many people have fought against rule by the Muslim north. Fighting in Darfur in western Sudan has caused great suffering.

EGYPT

Area: 386,662sq miles (1,001,449sq km)
Population: 78,887,000
Capital and largest city: Cairo
(pop 10,834,000)
Other large cities: Alexandria (3,917,000)
El Giza (2,492,000)
Official language: Arabic
Religions: Islam (90%), Christianity (10%)
Government: Republic
Currency: Egyptian pound

LIBYA

Area: 679,362sq miles (1,759,540sq km)
Population: 5,901,000
Capital and largest city: Tripoli
(pop 2,006,000)
Other large cities: Benghazi (681,000)
Official language: Arabic
Religion: Islam
Government: Republic
Currency: Libyan dinar

SUDAN

Area: 967,500sq miles (2,505,813sq km)
Population: 41,236,000
Capital and largest city: Khartoum
(pop 4,286,000)
Other large cities: Omdurman (3,128,000)
Khartoum North (1,726,000)
Official language: Arabic
Religions: Islam (75%), local religions (20%),
Christianity (5%)
Government: Republic
Currency: Sudanese dinar

Oilfields are found in the Sahara in central Libya. Pipelines carry the oil to the coast. Oil accounts for more than 90 percent of Libya's exports. Egypt produces only enough oil for its own needs.

Cotton is the chief cash crop in Egypt and Sudan. Both produce textiles, including clothes. Egypt also manufactures food products and vehicles. It is Africa's third most important industrial country after South Africa and Algeria.

Colonel Muammar Gaddafi and fellow military officers overthrew the king in Libya in 1969 and made Libya a republic. Gaddafi used money from oil exports to raise living standards in Libya. He has also given money to some overseas terrorist groups.

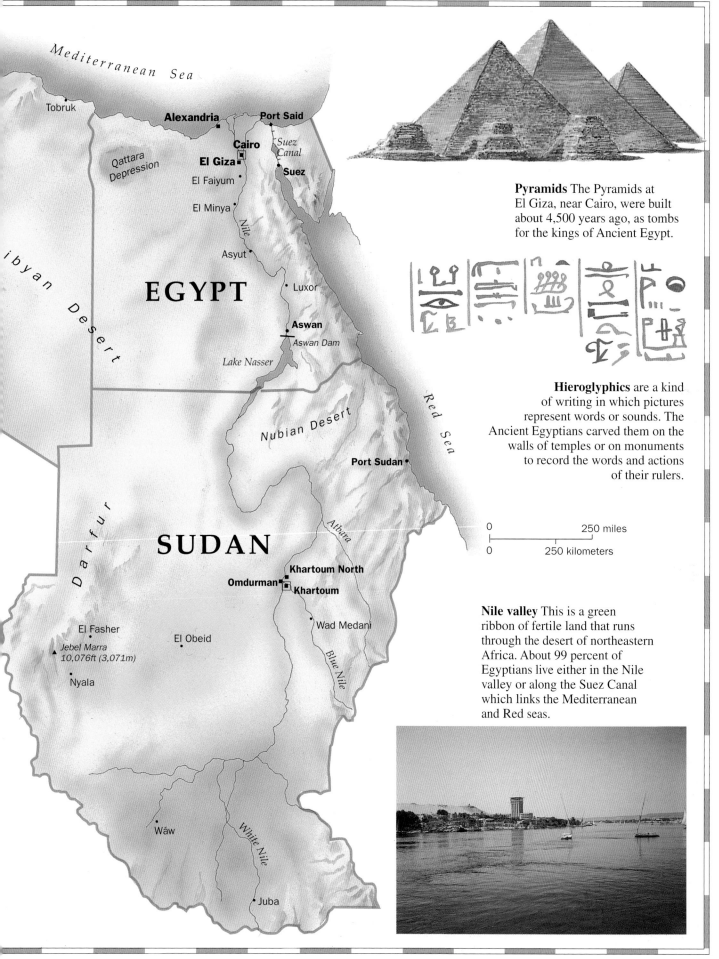

Mediterranean Sea

Tobruk

Alexandria

Port Said

Cairo

El Giza

Suez Canal

Suez

Qattara Depression

El Faiyum

El Minya

Nile

Asyut

Luxor

EGYPT

ibyan Desert

Aswan

Aswan Dam

Lake Nasser

Nubian Desert

Red Sea

Port Sudan

Athara

Darfur

SUDAN

Khartoum North

Omdurman

Khartoum

Wad Medani

El Fasher

El Obeid

Jebel Marra
10,076ft (3,071m)

Nyala

Blue Nile

Wáw

White Nile

Juba

Pyramids The Pyramids at El Giza, near Cairo, were built about 4,500 years ago, as tombs for the kings of Ancient Egypt.

Hieroglyphics are a kind of writing in which pictures represent words or sounds. The Ancient Egyptians carved them on the walls of temples or on monuments to record the words and actions of their rulers.

| 0 | 250 miles |
| 0 | 250 kilometers |

Nile valley This is a green ribbon of fertile land that runs through the desert of northeastern Africa. About 99 percent of Egyptians live either in the Nile valley or along the Suez Canal which links the Mediterranean and Red seas.

HORN OF AFRICA

Four countries – Eritrea, Ethiopia, Djibouti and
Somalia – are often called the Horn of Africa, because
they resemble the shape of a rhinoceros horn on a map.
Ethiopia is a mountainous country, with
rainforests in the southwest. But the lands of
northeastern and southeastern Ethiopia,
Eritrea, Djibouti and Somalia are largely
desert. All the countries are poor. They
have suffered in recent years from
droughts and civil wars.

ERITREA

Area: 36,170sq miles (93,680sq km)
Population: 4,787,000
Capital and largest city: Asmara (pop 556,000)
Official languages: Tigrinya, Arabic
Religions: Islam (50%), Christianity (50%)
Government: Republic
Currency: Nakfa

ETHIOPIA

Area: 435,608sq miles (1,128,220sq km)
Population: 74,778,000
Capital and largest city: Addis Ababa
(pop 2,723,000)
Official language: None (Amharic is used in
government)
Religions: Islam (45%), Christianity (35%),
local religions (11%)
Government: Republic
Currency: Birr

DJIBOUTI

Area: 8,494sq miles (22,000sq km)
Population: 721,000
Capital and largest city: Djibouti (pop 502,000)
Official languages: French, Arabic
Religion: Islam
Government: Republic
Currency: Djiboutian franc

SOMALIA

Area: 246,201sq miles (637,657sq km)
Population: 8,863,000
Capital and largest city: Mogadishu
(pop 1,175,000)
Official language: Somali
Religion: Islam
Government: Republic
Currency: Somalian franc

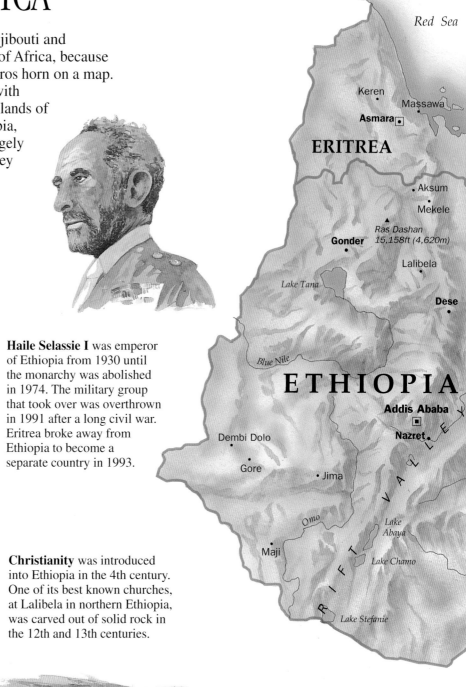

Haile Selassie I was emperor
of Ethiopia from 1930 until
the monarchy was abolished
in 1974. The military group
that took over was overthrown
in 1991 after a long civil war.
Eritrea broke away from
Ethiopia to become a
separate country in 1993.

Christianity was introduced
into Ethiopia in the 4th century.
One of its best known churches,
at Lalibela in northern Ethiopia,
was carved out of solid rock in
the 12th and 13th centuries.

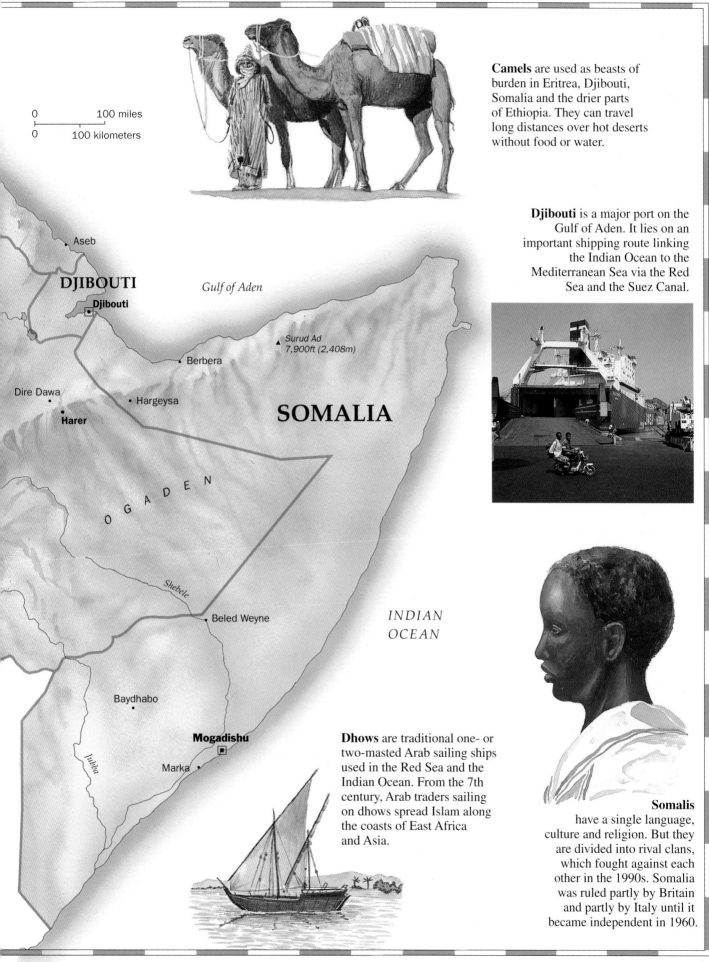

Camels are used as beasts of burden in Eritrea, Djibouti, Somalia and the drier parts of Ethiopia. They can travel long distances over hot deserts without food or water.

Djibouti is a major port on the Gulf of Aden. It lies on an important shipping route linking the Indian Ocean to the Mediterranean Sea via the Red Sea and the Suez Canal.

0   100 miles
0   100 kilometers

Aseb

DJIBOUTI

Djibouti

Gulf of Aden

Surud Ad
7,900ft (2,408m)

Berbera

Dire Dawa

Hargeysa

Harer

SOMALIA

O G A D E N

Shebele

Beled Weyne

INDIAN OCEAN

Baydhabo

Jubba

Mogadishu

Marka

Dhows are traditional one- or two-masted Arab sailing ships used in the Red Sea and the Indian Ocean. From the 7th century, Arab traders sailing on dhows spread Islam along the coasts of East Africa and Asia.

Somalis have a single language, culture and religion. But they are divided into rival clans, which fought against each other in the 1990s. Somalia was ruled partly by Britain and partly by Italy until it became independent in 1960.

11

WESTERN AFRICA 1

West Africa contains 15 countries (five of which are shown here). Desert covers much of Mauritania and Mali, but southern Mauritania and Mali, together with parts of Senegal and Burkina Faso, lie in a dry grassland region called the Sahel. To the south, the Sahel merges into savanna (tropical grassland with scattered trees). Forests grow along rivers. France once ruled Burkina Faso, Senegal, Mauritania and Mali. The Gambia was ruled by Britain until 1965.

MAURITANIA

Area: 397,956sq miles (1,030,700sq km)
Population: 3,177,000
Capital and largest city: Nouakchott (pop 600,000)
Official language: Arabic
Religion: Islam
Government: Islamic republic
Currency: Ouguiya

MALI

Area: 478,767sq miles (1,240,000sq km)
Population: 11,717,000
Capital and largest city: Bamako (pop 1,264,000)
Official language: French
Religions: Islam (90%), local religions (9%), Christianity (1%)
Government: Republic
Currency: CFA franc*

SENEGAL

Area: 75,750sq miles (196,192sq km)
Population: 11,987,000
Capital and largest city: Dakar (pop 2,167,000)
Official language: French
Religions: Islam (94%), Christianity (5%), local religions (1%)
Government: Republic
Currency: CFA franc

GAMBIA

Area: 4,361sq miles (11,295sq km)
Population: 1,642,000
Capital and largest city: Banjul (pop 372,000)
Official language: English
Religions: Islam (90%), Christianity (9%)
Government: Republic
Currency: Dalasi

Dakar is the capital of Senegal. It is a major port with a fine harbor and is one of Africa's leading industrial cities. The French founded Dakar in 1857 on the site of a fishing village.

Groundnuts are among Gambia's and Senegal's leading exports. In the five countries on this page, more than 80 percent of the people earn their living by farming.

BURKINA FASO

Area: 105,869sq miles (274,200sq km)
Population: 13,903,000
Capital and largest city: Ouagadougou (pop 821,000)
Official language: French
Religions: Islam (50%), local religions (40%), Christianity (10%)
Government: Republic
Currency: CFA franc

* CFA stands for Communautè Financière Africaine

ATLANTIC
OCEAN

• Nouadhibou

• Atâr

MAURITANIA

◻ Nouakchott

• St Louis

Dakar ◻

• Thiès

• Kaolack

SENEGAL

GAMBIA

Banjul ◻

Ziguinchor

Senegal

Gambia

Gambia is a popular holiday spot for tourists from northern Europe. It has good beaches and interesting places to visit on cruises up the Gambia River.

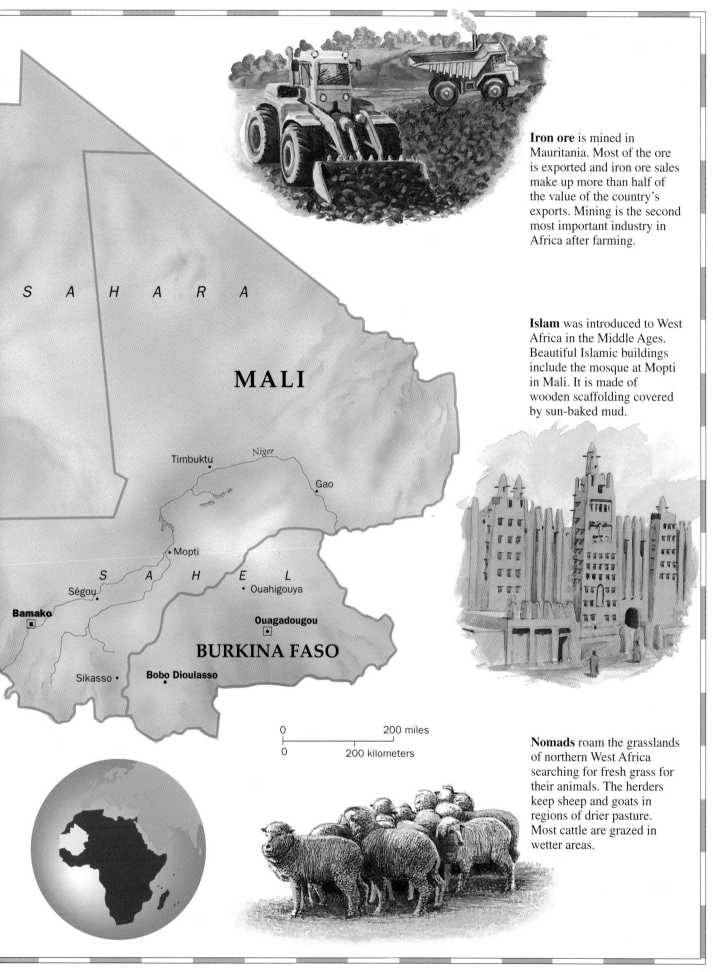

Iron ore is mined in Mauritania. Most of the ore is exported and iron ore sales make up more than half of the value of the country's exports. Mining is the second most important industry in Africa after farming.

Islam was introduced to West Africa in the Middle Ages. Beautiful Islamic buildings include the mosque at Mopti in Mali. It is made of wooden scaffolding covered by sun-baked mud.

SAHARA

MALI

Niger

Timbuktu

Gao

S A H E L

Mopti

Ségou

Ouahigouya

Bamako

Ouagadougou

BURKINA FASO

Sikasso

Bobo Dioulasso

| 0 | 200 miles |
| 0 | 200 kilometers |

Nomads roam the grasslands of northern West Africa searching for fresh grass for their animals. The herders keep sheep and goats in regions of drier pasture. Most cattle are grazed in wetter areas.

WESTERN AFRICA 2

The part of western Africa shown here includes four mainland countries and Cape Verde, a group of islands in the Atlantic Ocean, 400 miles (640km) west of Dakar. Liberia was founded by Americans in 1822 as a home for freed slaves, and became independent in 1847. Guinea was ruled by France until 1958, Sierra Leone by Britain until 1961. Guinea-Bissau and Cape Verde were ruled by Portugal until the mid-1970s.

 GUINEA

Area: 94,926sq miles (245,857sq km)
Population: 9,690,000
Capital and largest city: Conakry (pop 1,366,000)
Official language: French
Religions: Islam (85%), Christianity (8%), local religions (7%)
Government: Republic
Currency: Guinean franc

 GUINEA-BISSAU

Area: 13,948sq miles (36,125sq km)
Population: 1,442,000
Capital and largest city: Bissau (pop 336,000)
Official language: Portuguese
Religions: Local religions (50%), Islam (45%), Christianity (5%)
Government: Republic
Currency: CFA franc

 SIERRA LEONE

Area: 27,699sq miles (71,740sq km)
Population: 6,005,000
Capital and largest city: Freetown (pop 921,000)
Official language: English
Religions: Islam (60%), local religions (30%), Christianity (10%)
Government: Republic
Currency: Leone

 LIBERIA

Area: 43,000sq miles (111,369sq km)
Population: 3,042,000
Capital and largest city: Monrovia (pop 572,000)
Official language: English
Religions: Local religions (40%), Christianity (40%), Islam (20%)
Government: Republic
Currency: Liberian dollar

 **CAPE VERDE**

Area: 1,557sq miles (4,033sq km)
Population: 421,000
Capital and largest city: Praia (pop 107,000)
Official language: Portuguese
Religion: Christianity
Government: Republic
Currency: Escudo

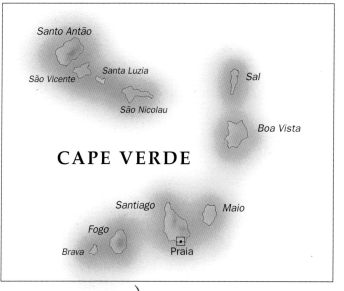

CAPE VERDE

Shrimp fishing is important in Guinea-Bissau, one of the world's poorest nations. It exports cashew nuts, shrimps, peanuts, palm kernels and timber. Cashew nuts account for more than four-fifths of its exports.

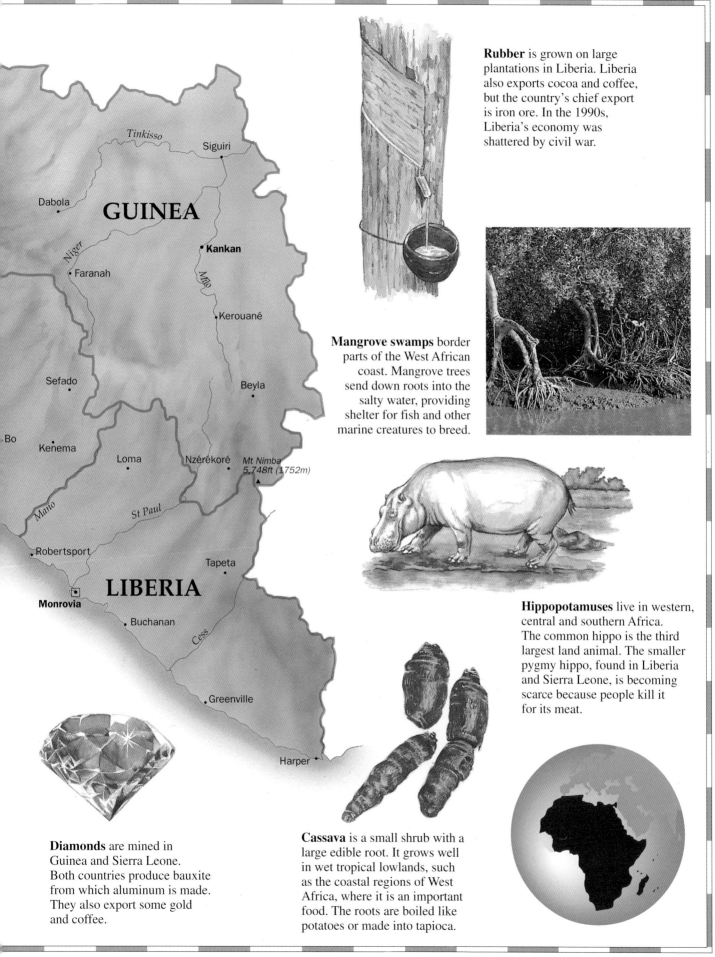

Rubber is grown on large plantations in Liberia. Liberia also exports cocoa and coffee, but the country's chief export is iron ore. In the 1990s, Liberia's economy was shattered by civil war.

Mangrove swamps border parts of the West African coast. Mangrove trees send down roots into the salty water, providing shelter for fish and other marine creatures to breed.

Hippopotamuses live in western, central and southern Africa. The common hippo is the third largest land animal. The smaller pygmy hippo, found in Liberia and Sierra Leone, is becoming scarce because people kill it for its meat.

Diamonds are mined in Guinea and Sierra Leone. Both countries produce bauxite from which aluminum is made. They also export some gold and coffee.

Cassava is a small shrub with a large edible root. It grows well in wet tropical lowlands, such as the coastal regions of West Africa, where it is an important food. The roots are boiled like potatoes or made into tapioca.

Map labels:
Tinkisso
Siguiri
Dabola
GUINEA
Kankan
Niger
Faranah
Milo
Kerouané
Sefado
Beyla
Bo
Kenema
Loma
Nzérékoré
Mt Nimba 5,748ft (1752m)
Mano
St Paul
Robertsport
Tapeta
LIBERIA
Monrovia
Buchanan
Cess
Greenville
Harper

WESTERN AFRICA 3

Five countries make up the eastern part of West Africa. One of them, Nigeria, has more people than any other African country. Nigeria and Ghana were formerly British territories, while Benin, Côte d'Ivoire (Ivory Coast) and Togo were ruled by France. Nearly half of the people in this part of West Africa earn their living by farming. Cocoa, coconuts and palm products, coffee and cotton are leading exports. Nigeria's main export is oil.

Cocoa beans, from which chocolate is made, are grown in West Africa. Côte d'Ivoire and Ghana are the world's leading producers, while Nigeria ranks fourth. Other major products include coffee, cotton, palm oil and palm kernels.

CÔTE D'IVOIRE

Area: 124,504sq miles (322,463sq km)
Population: 17,655,000
Capital: Yamoussoukro (pop 416,000)
Largest city: Abidjan (3,918,000)
Official language: French
Religions: Islam (40%), Christianity (30%), local religions (25%)
Government: Republic
Currency: CFA franc

GHANA

Area: 92,100sq miles (238,537sq km)
Population: 22,410,000
Capital and largest city: Accra (pop 1,847,000)
Official language: English
Religions: Christianity (63%), local religions (21%), Islam (16%)
Government: Republic
Currency: Cedi

TOGO

Area: 21,925sq miles (56,785sq km)
Population: 5,549,000
Capital and largest city: Lomé (pop 799,000)
Official language: French
Religions: Local religions (50%), Christianity (30%), Islam (20%)
Government: Republic
Currency: CFA franc

BENIN

Area: 43,484sq miles (112,622sq km)
Population: 7,863,000
Capital: Porto-Novo (pop 238,000)
Largest city: Cotonou (712,000)
Official language: French
Religions: Local religions (50%), Christianity (30%), Islam (20%)
Government: Republic
Currency: CFA franc

Korhogo

CÔTE D'IVOIRE

Man

Daloa

Bouaké

Lake Kossou

Yamoussoukro

Sassandra

Abidjan

Sassandra

Tabou

Comoé

White Volta

Tamale

GHANA

Kumasi

Lake Volta

Akosombo Dam

Accra

Cape Coast

Takoradi

ATLANTIC OCEAN

NIGERIA

Area: 356,669sq miles (923,768sq km)
Population: 131,860,000
Capital: Abuja (pop 452,000)
Largest city: Lagos (8,665,000)
Official language: English
Religions: Islam (50%), Christianity (40%), local religions (10%)
Government: Republic
Currency: Naira

Yamoussoukro, capital of Côte d'Ivoire, has the world's largest church, the Basilica of Our Lady of Peace, which was completed in 1989. The city was the birthplace of Félix Houphouët-Boigny, the country's president (1960-93).

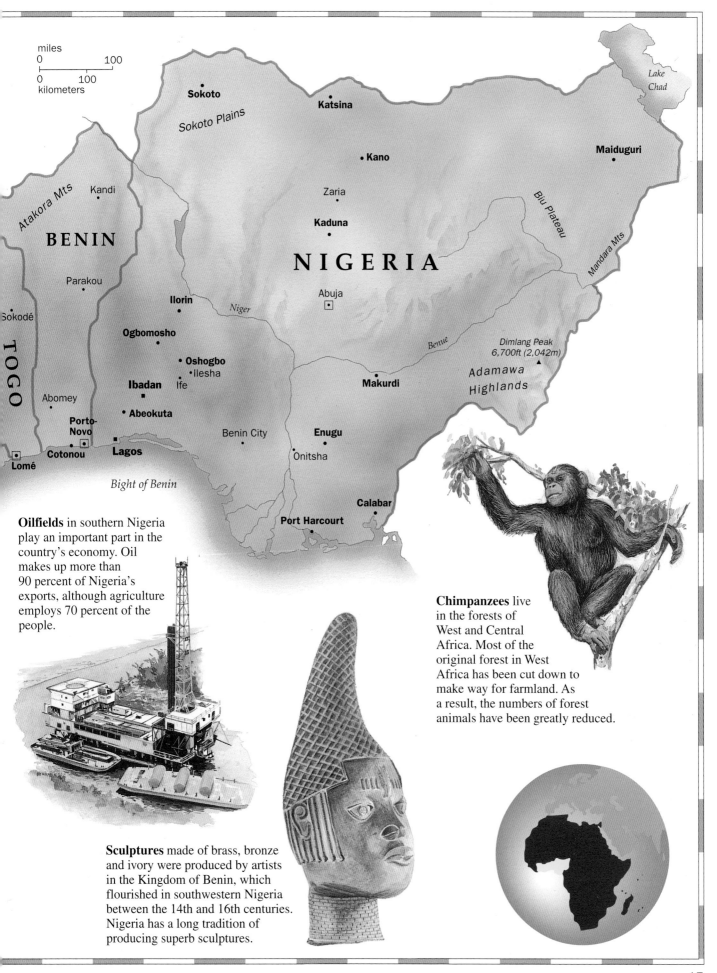

miles
0   100

kilometers
0   100

Sokoto

Katsina

Sokoto Plains

Kano

Lake Chad

Maiduguri

Kandi

Zaria

Atakora Mts

BENIN

Kaduna

NIGERIA

Biu Plateau

Mandara Mts

Parakou

Niger

Ilorin

Abuja

Sokodé

TOGO

Ogbomosho

Benue

Dimlang Peak
6,700ft (2,042m)

Oshogbo
•Ilesha

Ibadan   Ife

Makurdi

Adamawa Highlands

Abomey

Abeokuta

Porto-Novo

Benin City

Enugu

Cotonou

Onitsha

Lomé

Lagos

Bight of Benin

Calabar

Port Harcourt

Oilfields in southern Nigeria
play an important part in the
country's economy. Oil
makes up more than
90 percent of Nigeria's
exports, although agriculture
employs 70 percent of the
people.

Chimpanzees live
in the forests of
West and Central
Africa. Most of the
original forest in West
Africa has been cut down to
make way for farmland. As
a result, the numbers of forest
animals have been greatly reduced.

Sculptures made of brass, bronze
and ivory were produced by artists
in the Kingdom of Benin, which
flourished in southwestern Nigeria
between the 14th and 16th centuries.
Nigeria has a long tradition of
producing superb sculptures.

17

West-central Africa

Bordering Nigeria are two huge landlocked nations, Chad and Niger. Although Niger has some mineral resources, these two countries are among the world's poorest. Both contain large areas of desert and dry grassland, and crops are grown only in the south. Central African Republic, another landlocked country south of Chad, has grasslands in the north and forests in the south. Agriculture employs more than 80 percent of the people in this region.

NIGER

Area: 489,191sq miles (1,267,000sq km)
Population: 12,525,000
Capital: Niamey (pop 890,000)
Official language: French
Religions: Islam (80%), local religions and Christianity (20%)
Government: Republic
Currency: CFA franc

CHAD

Area: 495,755sq miles (1,284,000sq km)
Population: 9,944,000
Capital: N'Djamena (pop 797,000)
Official language: French
Religions: Islam (51%), Christianity (35%), local religions (7%)
Government: Republic
Currency: CFA franc

CENTRAL AFRICAN REPUBLIC

Area: 240,535sq miles (622,984sq km)
Population: 4,303,000
Capital: Bangui (pop 698,000)
Official language: French
Religions: Christianity (50%), local religions (35%), Islam (15%)
Government: Republic
Currency: CFA franc

SAHARA

Air Mts

NIGER

Agadez

Tahoua

Niamey

Maradi

Zinder

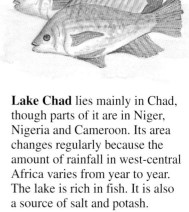

Deserts cover most of northern Chad and Niger. To the south, the deserts merge into the dry, grassy Sahel. When severe droughts occur, the Sahel becomes desert. When the rains return, the Sahel becomes green again.

Lake Chad lies mainly in Chad, though parts of it are in Niger, Nigeria and Cameroon. Its area changes regularly because the amount of rainfall in west-central Africa varies from year to year. The lake is rich in fish. It is also a source of salt and potash.

Niger was named after the Niger, one of Africa's longest rivers, which flows through southwestern Niger. Its waters are used to irrigate farmland. Southern Niger and Chad are covered by savanna.

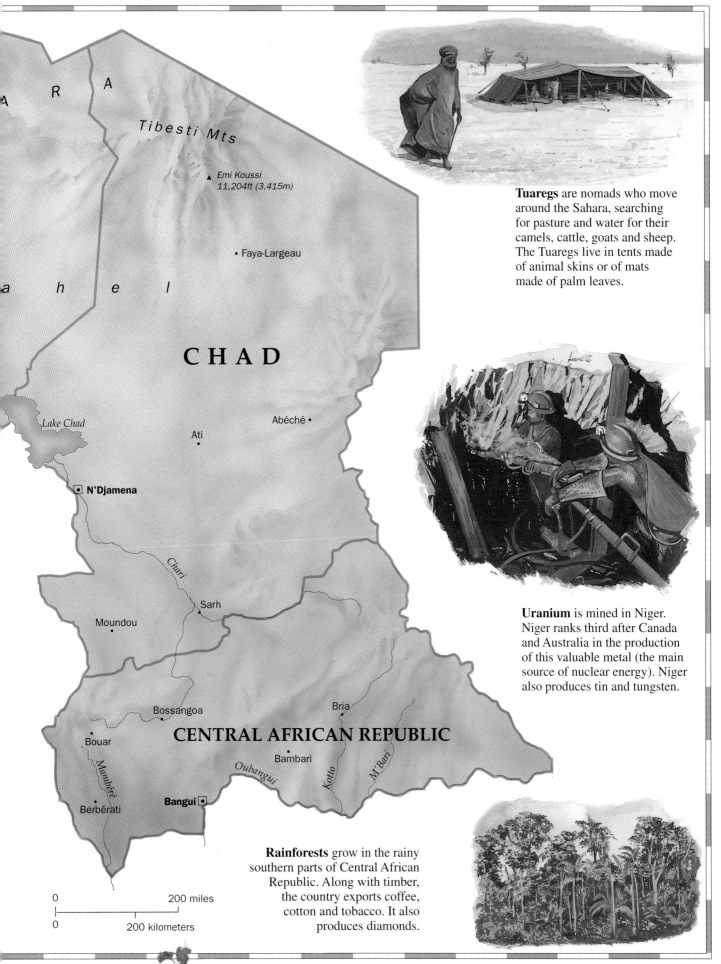

Tibesti Mts

▲ Emi Koussi
11,204ft (3,415m)

• Faya-Largeau

CHAD

Lake Chad

Abéché •

• Ati

☑ N'Djamena

Chari

• Sarh

Moundou •

Bossangoa •

• Bria

Bouar •

CENTRAL AFRICAN REPUBLIC

• Bambari

Mambéré

Oubangui

Kotto

M'Bari

Berbérati •

Bangui ☑

Tuaregs are nomads who move around the Sahara, searching for pasture and water for their camels, cattle, goats and sheep. The Tuaregs live in tents made of animal skins or of mats made of palm leaves.

Uranium is mined in Niger. Niger ranks third after Canada and Australia in the production of this valuable metal (the main source of nuclear energy). Niger also produces tin and tungsten.

Rainforests grow in the rainy southern parts of Central African Republic. Along with timber, the country exports coffee, cotton and tobacco. It also produces diamonds.

0   200 miles

0   200 kilometers

CENTRAL AFRICA 1

Four tropical countries – Cameroon, Republic of Congo, Equatorial Guinea and Gabon – lie between Nigeria and the huge Democratic Republic of Congo. Equatorial Guinea contains an area on the mainland and a volcanic island, Bioko, which contains its capital. South of Bioko lies the islan d nation of São Tomé and Pñcipe. Most people in these countries work on farms. Congo and Gabon have important oil deposits.

CAMEROON

Area: 183,569sq miles (475,442sq km)
Population: 17,341,000
Capital: Yaoundé (pop1,616,000)
Official languages: English, French
Religions: Christianity (40%), local religions (40%), Islam (20%)
Government: Republic
Currency: CFA franc

CONGO, REPUBLIC OF

Area: 132,047sq miles (342,000sq km)
Population: 3,702,000
Capital: Brazzaville (pop 1,080,000)
Official language: French
Religions: Christianity (50%), local religions (40%), Islam (2%)
Government: Republic
Currency: CFA franc

EQUATORIAL GUINEA

Area: 10,831sq miles (28,051sq km)
Population: 540,000
Capital: Malabo (pop 95,000)
Official languages: Spanish, French
Religions: Christianity (89%), local religions (5%)
Government: Republic
Currency: CFA franc

GABON

Area: 103,347sq miles (267,667sq km)
Population: 1,425,000
Capital: Libreville (pop 611,000)
Official language: French
Religions: Christianity (80%), local religions (19%), Islam (1%)
Government: Republic
Currency: CFA franc

Soccer is a popular sport throughout Africa. National teams from Africa that have made their mark in international soccer competitions include Cameroon, Nigeria and Ghana.

Plantains are a large kind of banana. They are grown throughout West and Central Africa, where they are eaten as a vegetable. The leaves are used to make bags or mats and sometimes for roofing houses.

SÃO TOMÉ AND PRINCIPE

Area: 372sq miles (964sq km)
Population: 193,000
Capital: São Tomé (pop 54,000)
Official language: Portuguese
Religion: Christianity
Government: Republic
Currency: Dobra

ATLANTIC OCEAN

SÃO TOMÉ AND PRINCIPE

São Tomé

São Tomé

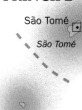

Annobón (Equat. Gui)

Libreville, capital of Gabon, is a major port. Its name means "free town," and its origins are similar to those of Liberia. Libreville was founded by French officers in 1849 as a home for freed slaves.

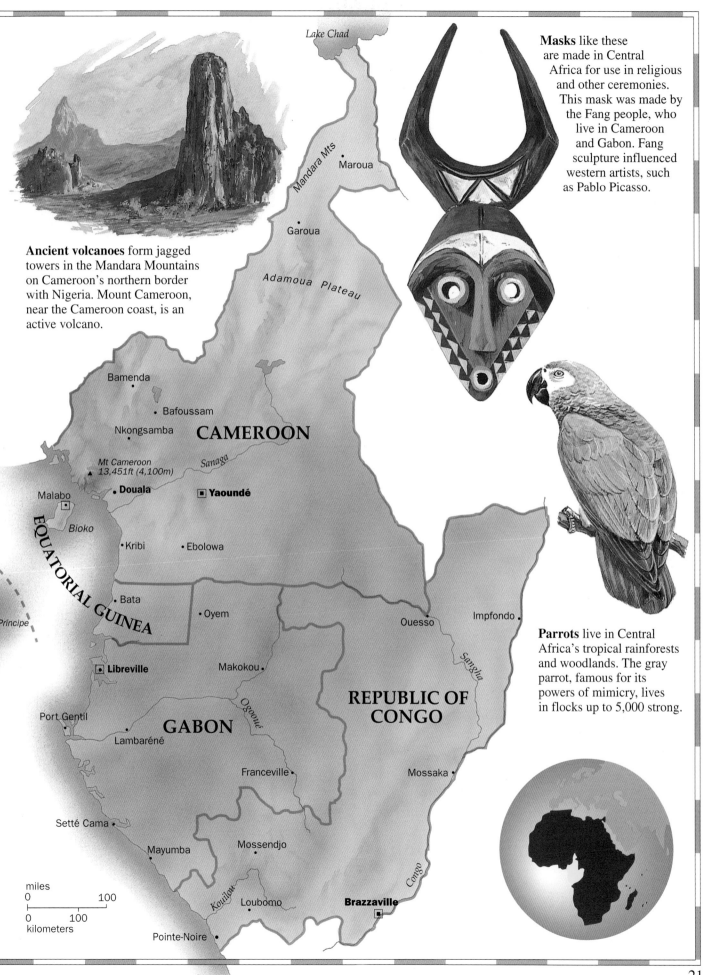

Masks like these are made in Central Africa for use in religious and other ceremonies. This mask was made by the Fang people, who live in Cameroon and Gabon. Fang sculpture influenced western artists, such as Pablo Picasso.

Ancient volcanoes form jagged towers in the Mandara Mountains on Cameroon's northern border with Nigeria. Mount Cameroon, near the Cameroon coast, is an active volcano.

Parrots live in Central Africa's tropical rainforests and woodlands. The gray parrot, famous for its powers of mimicry, lives in flocks up to 5,000 strong.

Lake Chad

Mandara Mts

Maroua

Garoua

Adamoua Plateau

Bamenda

Bafoussam

Nkongsamba

CAMEROON

Sanaga

Mt Cameroon
▲ 13,451ft (4,100m)

Malabo

Douala

■ **Yaoundé**

Bioko

Kribi

Ebolowa

EQUATORIAL GUINEA

Bata

Oyem

Ouesso

Impfondo

Sangha

Príncipe

■ **Libreville**

Makokou

REPUBLIC OF CONGO

Port Gentil

Ogooué

GABON

Lambaréné

Franceville

Mossaka

Setté Cama

Mossendjo

Mayumba

Koulou

miles
0   100
0   100
kilometers

Loubomo

Congo

Brazzaville

Pointe-Noire

CENTRAL AFRICA 2

The Democratic Republic of Congo, called Zaire from 1971 to 1997, is Africa's third largest country after Sudan and Algeria. It was ruled by Belgium until 1960, when the country was plunged into civil war between rival ethnic groups. The army leader General Mobutu restored order, but he became a dictator. Mobutu was overthrown in 1997, but the conflicts continued. Burundi and Rwanda have also suffered civil wars between two groups, the Hutus and Tutsis.

CONGO, DEMOCRATIC REPUBLIC OF

Area: 905,568sq miles (2,345,409sq km)
Population: 62,661,000
Capital and largest city: Kinshasa (pop 5,227,000)
Other large cities: Lubumbashi (1,485,000) Mbuji Mayi (919,000)
Official language: French
Religions: Christianity (70%), Islam (10%), local religions (10%)
Government: Republic
Currency: Congolese franc

BURUNDI

Area: 10,747sq miles (27,834sq km)
Population: 8,090,000
Capital: Bujumbura (pop 378,000)
Official languages: Kirundi, French
Government: Republic
Currency: Burundian franc

RWANDA

Area: 10,169sq miles (26,338sq km)
Population: 8,648,000
Capital: Kigali (pop 656,000)
Official languages: Kinyarwanda, French
Government: Republic
Currency: Rwandan franc

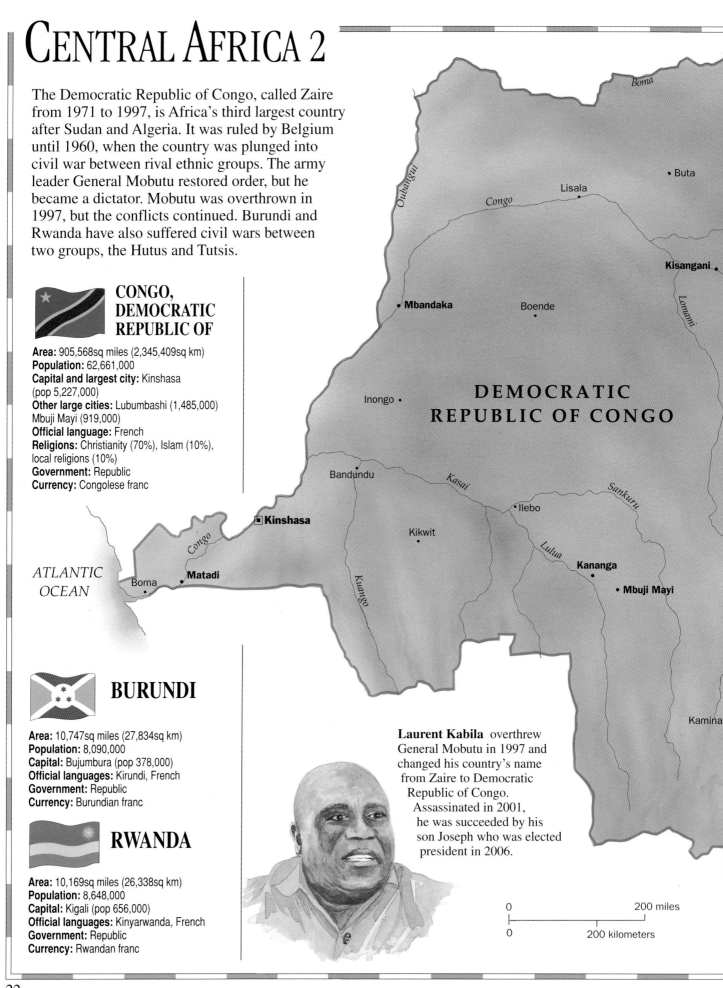

DEMOCRATIC REPUBLIC OF CONGO

ATLANTIC OCEAN

Laurent Kabila overthrew General Mobutu in 1997 and changed his country's name from Zaire to Democratic Republic of Congo. Assassinated in 2001, he was succeeded by his son Joseph who was elected president in 2006.

0 — 200 miles
0 — 200 kilometers

Congo is also the name of the world's fifth longest river. Called the Zaire from 1971 to 1997, the river has more water than any other apart from the Amazon in South America. It is a major route for carrying goods through the dense rainforest.

Pygmies live in small groups in the forests of Central Africa. From around 100 BCE, people from the Cameroon area, who spoke Bantu languages, began to settle in Central Africa. They pushed the Pygmies into remote areas. Bantu-speaking people now occupy most of Central, East and Southern Africa.

Mountain gorillas live in Rwanda and in the mountains to the west. Their survival in Rwanda was threatened in the 1990s by fighting in the area where they live. Conflict between Hutus and Tutsis caused great loss of life and harmed the economies of Burundi and Rwanda.

Mining is a major industry in the Democratic Republic of Congo, which leads the world in mining industrial diamonds. It also produces copper, cobalt, manganese, silver and tin. Some oil is obtained off the coast.

Coffee dominates the exports of both Burundi and Rwanda. The two war-shattered countries rank among the ten poorest in the world. Manufacturing and mining are on a small scale.

Isiro

Aruwimi

Lake Albert

Margherita Peak
16,765ft (5,110m)

Lake Edward

RWANDA

Lake Kivu

Kigali

Bukavu

Kindu

Bujumbura

BURUNDI

Lualaba

Lake Tanganyika

Kabalo

Kalemie

Lake Mweru

M i t u m b a   M t s

Katanga

Likasi

olwezi

Lubumbashi

EAST AFRICA

East Africa consists of three countries that were formerly ruled by Britain. Although the region lies on the equator, much of it is high tableland where the weather is much more pleasant than on the hot and humid coast. All three countries have large national parks, where visitors can see a wide variety of wildlife at close range. More than 70 percent of the people live by farming. The main products include coffee, cotton and tea.

UGANDA

Area: 91,134sq miles (236,036sq km)
Population: 28,196,000
Capital: Kampala (pop 1,246,000)
Official language: English
Religions: Christianity (66%), local religions (18%), Islam (16%)
Government: Republic
Currency: Ugandan shilling

KENYA

Area: 224,961sq miles (582,646sq km)
Population: 34,708,000
Capital: Nairobi (pop 2,575,000)
Official languages: Swahili, English
Religions: Christianity (80%), Islam (10%), local religions (10%)
Government: Republic
Currency: Kenyan shilling

TANZANIA

Area: 364,900sq miles (945,087sq km)
Population: 37,445,000
Capital: Dodoma (pop 155,000)
Official languages: Swahili, English
Religions: Islam (35%), local religions (35%), Christianity (30%)
Government: Republic
Currency: Tanzanian shilling

Lake Victoria is Africa's largest lake and also the world's second largest freshwater lake after Lake Superior in North America. One of the main sources of the River Nile, it was named after Queen Victoria.

Kilimanjaro in northern Tanzania is Africa's highest mountain. It is an extinct volcano. Early European explorers were amazed to find a snow-capped mountain so close to the equator.

Serengeti National Park, in northern Tanzania, covers 5,600sq miles (14,500sq km). It contains many animals, such as zebras, buffaloes, elephants, gazelles, giraffes, leopards and lions. Many tourists visit East Africa to see the wonderful wildlife.

Olduvai Gorge is a site in northern Tanzania where the fossils of ancient human-like creatures have been found, together with the tools they used. Many scientists believe that the first true humans evolved in East Africa.

Masai herders live in Kenya and Tanzania. Kenya has about 40 groups of people and Tanzania 120. Each group has its own language, but most speak a second language, Swahili, so that they can talk to people from other groups.

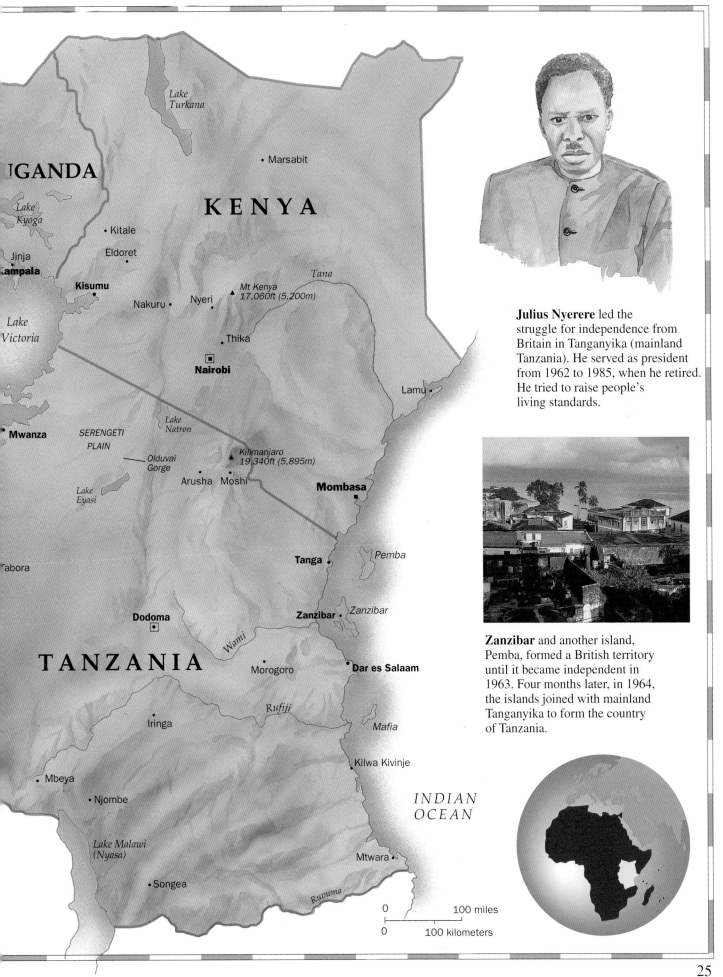

Lake Turkana

UGANDA

Lake Kyoga

Jinja

Kampala

Kisumu

Nakuru

Lake Victoria

Mwanza

SERENGETI PLAIN

Olduvai Gorge

Lake Eyasi

Tabora

KENYA

Marsabit

Kitale

Eldoret

Nyeri

▲ Mt Kenya 17,060ft (5,200m)

Tana

Thika

■ **Nairobi**

Lake Natron

Arusha Moshi

Kilimanjaro ▲ 19,340ft (5,895m)

Lamu

Mombasa ■

Tanga

Pemba

Zanzibar Zanzibar

Dodoma ⊡

Wami

TANZANIA

Morogoro

Dar es Salaam

Rufiji

Mafia

Iringa

Kilwa Kivinje

Mbeya

Njombe

INDIAN OCEAN

Lake Malawi (Nyasa)

Mtwara

Songea

Ruvuma

Julius Nyerere led the struggle for independence from Britain in Tanganyika (mainland Tanzania). He served as president from 1962 to 1985, when he retired. He tried to raise people's living standards.

Zanzibar and another island, Pemba, formed a British territory until it became independent in 1963. Four months later, in 1964, the islands joined with mainland Tanganyika to form the country of Tanzania.

| 0 | 100 miles |
| 0 | 100 kilometers |

INDIAN OCEAN TERRITORIES

Four independent island countries in the Indian Ocean are considered to be part of the African continent. They are Madagascar, which is by far the largest, Comoros, Mauritius and Seychelles. The French island of Réunion, east of Madagascar, is also part of Africa. Madagascar is unusual. Its people are a mixture of Indonesian and black African people. Its chief language, Malagasy, resembles Malay and Indonesian.

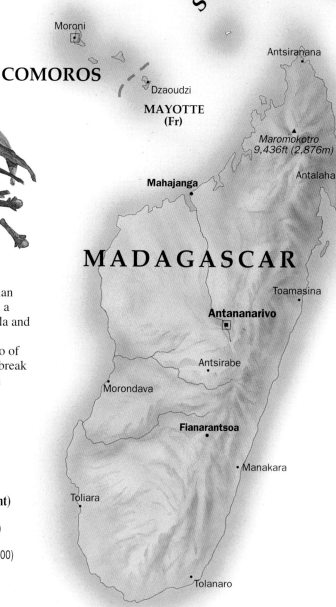

Lemurs, a name meaning "ghosts," are primates that live on Madagascar and the Comoros. They evolved over the last 60 million years, when the islands were cut off from mainland Africa.

SEYCHELLES

Area: 156sq miles (404sq km)
Population: 82,000
Capital: Victoria (pop 25,000)
Official language: None
Religions: Christianity (96%), Hinduism (2%), Islam (1%)
Government: Republic
Currency: Seychelles rupee

COMOROS

Area: 838sq miles (2,171sq km)
Population: 691,000
Capital: Moroni (pop 53,000)
Official languages: Arabic, French, Comoran
Religions: Islam (98%), Christianity (2%)
Government: Republic
Currency: Comoran franc

MADAGASCAR

Area: 226,658sq miles (587,041sq km)
Population: 18,595,000
Capital: Antananarivo (pop 1,678,000)
Official languages: Malagasy, French
Religions: Local religions (52%), Christianity (41%), Islam (7%)
Government: Republic
Currency: Madagascar ariary

MAURITIUS

Area: 720sq miles (1,865sq km)
Population: 1,241,000
Capital: Port Louis (pop 143,000)
Languages: English (official), Creole
Religions: Hinduism (48%), Christianity (32%), Islam (16%)
Government: Republic
Currency: Mauritian rupee

REUNION

(French overseas department)

Area: 969sq miles (2,510sq km)
Population: 788,000
Capital: Saint-Denis (pop 138,000)
Official language: French
Religion: Christianity (86%)
Government: Republic
Currency: Euro

Spices are grown on Indian Ocean islands. Comoros, a producer of cloves, vanilla and perfume oils, became independent in 1975. Two of the three islands tried to break away from the country in 1997-8.

■ Victoria
Mahé

Turtles, like this leatherback, come on shore in the Seychelles and other islands to lay their eggs. Hunted for food and for their shells, they are now an endangered species – though there are no reliable records of their numbers.

INDIAN OCEAN

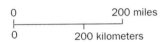
| 0 | 200 miles |
| 0 | 200 kilometers |

Tourism is the chief activity of people in the Seychelles, which has many beautiful beaches. Tourism is also important on other islands, especially Mauritius and Madagascar.

Rice is the chief food crop in Madagascar. Historians believe that rice-growing was introduced to Madagascar by people from Southeast Asia who settled on the island. Coffee is Madagascar's leading export.

MAURITIUS

Port Louis ▣

Saint-Denis ▣

REUNION (Fr)

Sugar cane is the leading crop and one of the chief exports of Mauritius. Most of it is grown on large plantations. Sugar production employs about one-third of all workers on the island.

SOUTHEASTERN AFRICA

Southeastern Africa consists of two former British territories – Malawi and Swaziland – and the former Portuguese territory of Mozambique. Malawi became independent in 1964 and Swaziland in 1968. Mozambique achieved independence in 1975. A civil war then occurred as a rebel force, supported by the white governments in Rhodesia (now Zimbabwe) and South Africa, fought to overthrow the government. Many people died. The civil war in Mozambique officially ended in 1992.

MALAWI

Area: 45,747sq miles (118,484sq km)
Population: 13,014,000
Capital: Lilongwe (pop 587,000)
Official language: Chichewa
Religions: Christianity (80%), Islam (13%), local religions (3%)
Government: Republic
Currency: Kwacha

MOZAMBIQUE

Area: 309,496sq miles (801,590sq km)
Population: 19,687,000
Capital: Maputo (pop 1,221,000)
Official language: Portuguese
Religions: Christianity (39%), Islam (17%), local religions (17%)
Government: Republic
Currency: Metical

SWAZILAND

Area: 6,704sq miles (17,363sq km)
Population: 1,136,000
Capital: Mbabane (pop 70,000)
Official languages: Swazi, English
Religions: Christianity (60%), local religions (30%), Islam (10%)
Government: Monarchy
Currency: Lilangeni

Hastings Kamuzu Banda led the independence struggle in Malawi. After independence in 1964, he became prime minister and later president, but he became increasingly arrogant, suppressing all opposition. He was defeated in elections in 1994 and died in 1997.

Lake Malawi occupies part of the Great Rift Valley. This deep valley runs from southeastern Africa, through East Africa and Ethiopia to the Red Sea. It continues into southwestern Asia, where it contains the Dead Sea.

Hydroelectricity is produced at the Cabora Bassa Dam on the Zambezi River in western Mozambique. Coal and oil are in short supply in much of southern Africa. Hydroelectric plants are major sources of electricity.

Pineapples are an important crop in Swaziland, together with citrus fruits, cotton, rice, sugar cane and tobacco. Swaziland has a varied economy. It is one of the few countries in Africa that exports more than it imports.

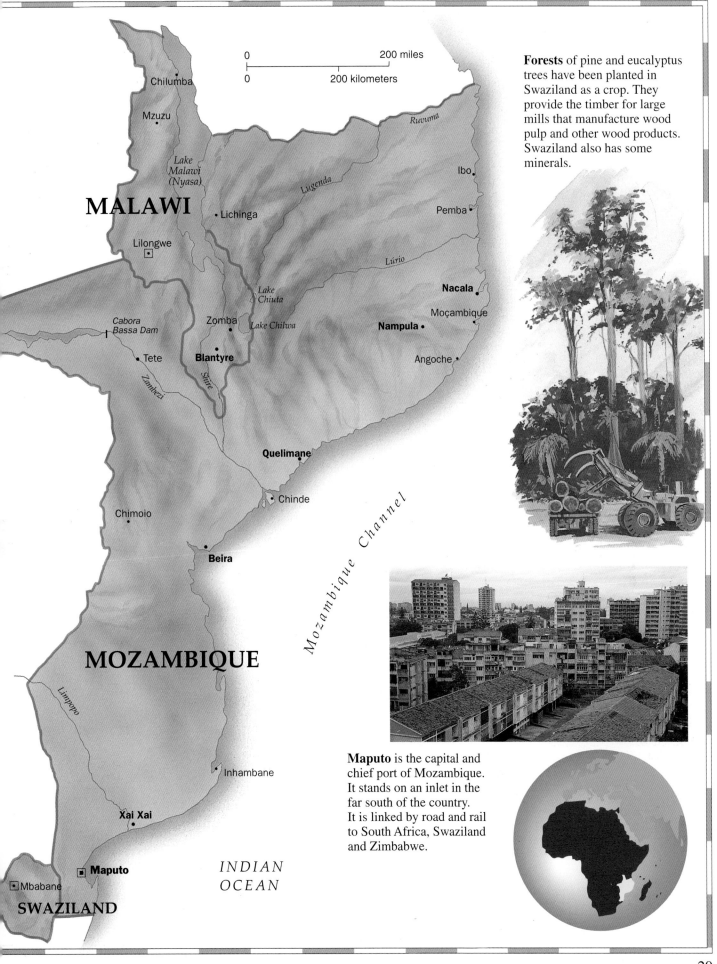

0 | 200 miles
0 | 200 kilometers

Chilumba

Mzuzu

Ruvuma

Ibo

Lake Malawi (Nyasa)

MALAWI

Lugenda

Lichinga

Pemba

Lilongwe

Lúrio

Nacala

Lake Chiuta

Moçambique

Zomba

Lake Chilwa

Nampula

Cabora Bassa Dam

Zambezi

Tete

Blantyre

Shire

Angoche

Quelimane

Chinde

Chimoio

Mozambique Channel

Beira

MOZAMBIQUE

Limpopo

Inhambane

Xai Xai

Maputo

INDIAN
OCEAN

Mbabane

SWAZILAND

Forests of pine and eucalyptus trees have been planted in Swaziland as a crop. They provide the timber for large mills that manufacture wood pulp and other wood products. Swaziland also has some minerals.

Maputo is the capital and chief port of Mozambique. It stands on an inlet in the far south of the country. It is linked by road and rail to South Africa, Swaziland and Zimbabwe.

SOUTH-CENTRAL AFRICA

Two large landlocked countries – Zambia and Zimbabwe – lie at the heart of southern Africa. Zambia is a former British territory that was called Northern Rhodesia before it became independent in 1964. Zimbabwe, another former British territory, was formerly called Southern Rhodesia and then, from 1964 to 1980, Rhodesia. Both countries have important mineral resources, but agriculture still employs about 70 percent of the people.

Beef cattle were reared on large, mostly white-owned, ranches in Zimbabwe. When the farmland was redistributed to local farmers, production levels of meat and dairy products dropped. Arable crops, including corn, the chief crop in both Zimbabwe and Zambia, also diminished.

ZAMBIA

Area: 290,586sq miles (752,614sq km)
Population: 11,502,000
Capital and largest city: Lusaka (pop 1,394,000)
Other large cities: Kitwe (416,000)
Ndola (402,000)
Kabwe (193,000)
Chingola (148,000)
Official language: English
Religions: Christianity (50%), Islam (20%), Hinduism (20%)
Government: Republic
Currency: Kwacha

ZIMBABWE

Area: 150,804sq miles (390,580sq km)
Population: 12,237,000
Capital and largest city: Harare (pop 1,469,000)
Other large cities: Bulawayo (713,000)
Chitungwiza (352,000)
Mutare (194,000)
Gweru (149,000)
Official language: English
Religions: Christianity (45%), local religions (40%)
Government: Republic
Currency: Zimbabwean dollar

Copper is mined in a region called the Copperbelt in northern Zambia, along the border with the Democratic Republic of Congo. Copper accounts for about 50 percent of Zambia's exports.

Great Zimbabwe is a historic site in Zimbabwe that contains the ruins of impressive stone buildings. It was capital of a Shona kingdom that flourished between the Limpopo and Zambezi rivers between about 1250 and 1450.

Kasempa

Zambezi

Mongu

Sesheke

Livingstone

Victoria Falls

Tobacco is a major export from Zimbabwe and the country ranks sixth among the world's tobacco producers. Zimbabwe also exports maize and cotton. Zambia also produces some tobacco.

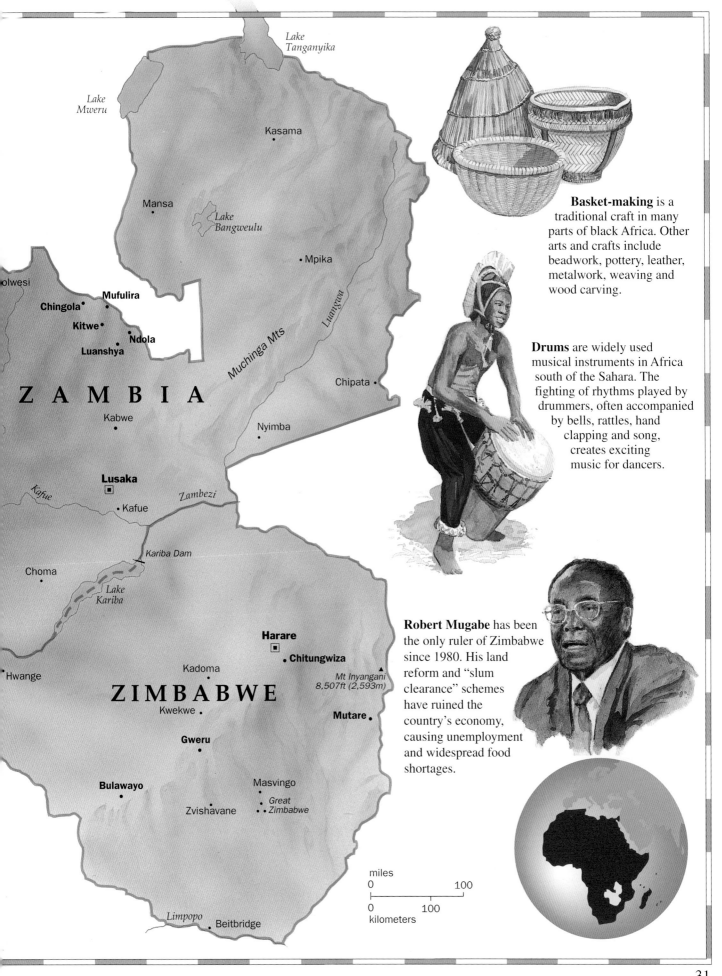

Lake
Tanganyika

Lake
Mweru

Kasama

Mansa

Lake
Bangweulu

Mpika

olwesi

Mufulira

Chingola

Kitwe **Ndola**

Luanshya

Muchinga Mts

Luangua

Chipata

Z A M B I A

Kabwe

Nyimba

Lusaka

Kafue

Kafue

Zambezi

Kariba Dam

Choma

Lake
Kariba

Harare

Chitungwiza

Hwange

Kadoma

Mt Inyangani
8,507ft (2,593m)

Z I M B A B W E

Kwekwe

Mutare

Gweru

Bulawayo

Masvingo

Zvishavane

Great
Zimbabwe

Limpopo

Beitbridge

Basket-making is a traditional craft in many parts of black Africa. Other arts and crafts include beadwork, pottery, leather, metalwork, weaving and wood carving.

Drums are widely used musical instruments in Africa south of the Sahara. The fighting of rhythms played by drummers, often accompanied by bells, rattles, hand clapping and song, creates exciting music for dancers.

Robert Mugabe has been the only ruler of Zimbabwe since 1980. His land reform and "slum clearance" schemes have ruined the country's economy, causing unemployment and widespread food shortages.

miles
0   100

0   100
kilometers

SOUTHWESTERN AFRICA

Southwestern Africa consists of Angola and Namibia on the Atlantic Ocean coast, and Botswana, a landlocked country that borders Namibia. Botswana is a former British territory that became independent in 1966. Angola became independent from Portugal in 1975, but it then suffered a long civil war. Namibia, formerly called South West Africa, became independent from South Africa in 1990. All three countries are rich in diamonds and other minerals.

Corn is an important part of the diet of many black Africans in southern Africa. It contains starch, which provides the body with energy, but it lacks many other nutrients the body needs. People who depend on it may suffer from malnutrition.

ANGOLA

Area: 481,354sq miles (1,246,700sq km)
Population: 12,127,000
Capital: Luanda (pop 2,623,000)
Official language: Portuguese
Religions: Christianity (50%), local religions (47%)
Government: Republic
Currency: Kwanza

BOTSWANA

Area: 224,607sq miles (581,730sq km)
Population: 1,640,000
Capital: Gaborone (pop 199,000)
Languages: Setswana, English (official)
Religions: Christianity (70%), local religions (10%)
Government: Republic
Currency: Pula

NAMIBIA

Area: 318,261sq miles (824,292sq km)
Population: 2,044,000
Capital: Windhoek (pop 237,000)
Official language: English
Religions: Christianity (80%), local religions (20%)
Government: Republic
Currency: Namibian dollar

Wood carving is one of the leading art forms in black Africa. Carvings of chiefs and heroes by the Chokwe people of Angola, made over the last 200 years, are found in museums all round the world. But wood is perishable and few older carvings have survived.

Sand dunes form towering hills in the Namib Desert, which stretches along the western coast of Namibia. Most of the little water it gets comes from mists that roll in from the sea.

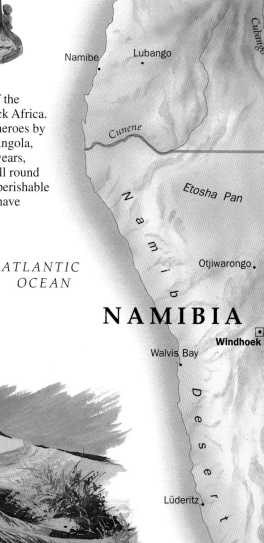

CABINDA
(Angola)
Cabinda

Luanda
Malanje
Cuanza

ANGOLA

Lobito
*Serra Moco
8,593ft (2,619m)*
Benguela
Huambo

Namibe
Lubango
Cubango

Cunene

N
a
m
i
b

Etosha Pan

*ATLANTIC
OCEAN*

Otjiwarongo

NAMIBIA
Windhoek
Walvis Bay

D
e
s
e
r
t

Lüderitz

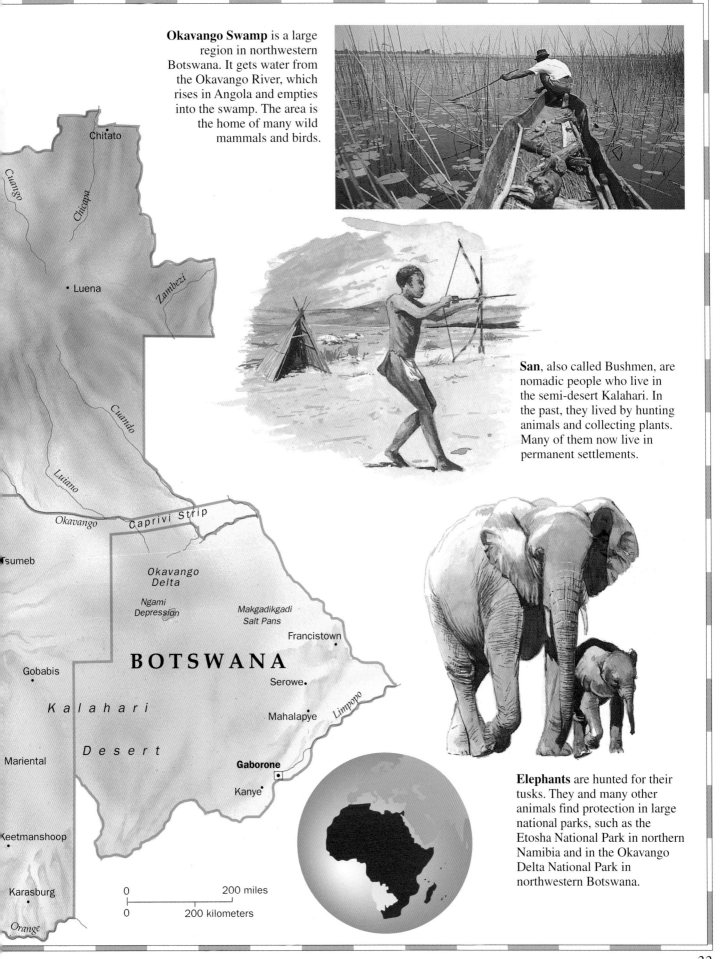

Okavango Swamp is a large region in northwestern Botswana. It gets water from the Okavango River, which rises in Angola and empties into the swamp. The area is the home of many wild mammals and birds.

San, also called Bushmen, are nomadic people who live in the semi-desert Kalahari. In the past, they lived by hunting animals and collecting plants. Many of them now live in permanent settlements.

Elephants are hunted for their tusks. They and many other animals find protection in large national parks, such as the Etosha National Park in northern Namibia and in the Okavango Delta National Park in northwestern Botswana.

Chitato

Cuango

Chicapa

Luena

Zambezi

Cuando

Luiano

Okavango

Caprivi Strip

Tsumeb

Okavango Delta

Ngami Depression

Makgadikgadi Salt Pans

Francistown

BOTSWANA

Gobabis

Serowe

Mariental

K a l a h a r i

D e s e r t

Mahalapye

Limpopo

Gaborone

Kanye

Keetmanshoop

Karasburg

Orange

| 0 | | 200 miles |
| 0 | | 200 kilometers |

SOUTHERN AFRICA

South Africa and Lesotho occupy the southern tip of Africa. South Africa is Africa's most developed country, though most of its black people are poor. In 1948, the South African government introduced a policy called apartheid, under which non-whites had no votes and strictly limited human rights. But multiracial elections in 1994 produced a government and equal rights for all the people of South Africa.

Gold mining is important in South Africa, which leads the world in gold production. The country also produces coal, chromite, copper, diamonds, iron ore, manganese, platinum and uranium. South Africa is also the most industrialized country in the continent.

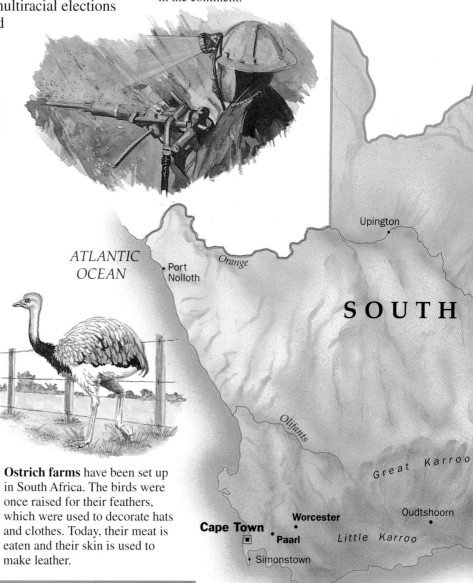

 SOUTH AFRICA

Area: 471,445sq miles (1,221,037sq km)
Population: 44,188,000
Capitals: Tshwane, formerly Pretoria (administrative), Cape Town (legislative), Bloemfontein (judicial)
Largest cities: Cape Town (pop 2,967,000)
Johannesburg (2,732,000)
Durban (2,370,000)
Soweto (1,839,000)
Tshwane (1,209,000)
Port Elizabeth (1,018,000)
Official languages: Zulu, Xhosa, Afrikaans, Sepedi, English, Setswana, Sesotho, Xitsonga, Ndebele, Swati, Tshivenda
Religions: Christianity (80%), local religions (5%), Islam (2%)
Government: Republic
Currency: Rand

 LESOTHO

Area: 11,720sq miles (30,355sq km)
Population: 2,022,000
Capital: Maseru (pop 170,000)
Official languages: English, Sesotho, Zulu, Xhosa
Religions: Christianity (80%), local religions (20%)
Government: Monarchy
Currency: Loti

ATLANTIC OCEAN

Ostrich farms have been set up in South Africa. The birds were once raised for their feathers, which were used to decorate hats and clothes. Today, their meat is eaten and their skin is used to make leather.

Upington

Port Nolloth

Orange

SOUTH

Olifants

Great Karroo

Oudtshoorn

Worcester

Cape Town
Paarl

Little Karroo

Simonstown

Table Mountain is a flat-topped upland that overlooks Cape Town and Table Bay, in southwestern South Africa. Cloud often covers the top of Table Mountain and spills over the edge like a tablecloth.

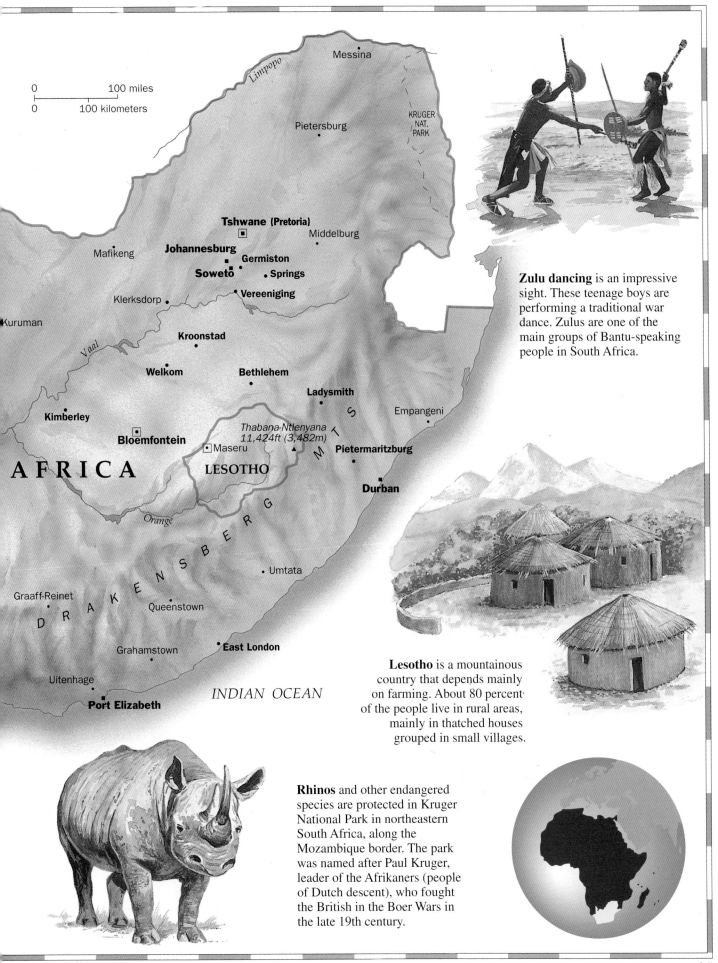

Zulu dancing is an impressive sight. These teenage boys are performing a traditional war dance. Zulus are one of the main groups of Bantu-speaking people in South Africa.

Lesotho is a mountainous country that depends mainly on farming. About 80 percent of the people live in rural areas, mainly in thatched houses grouped in small villages.

Rhinos and other endangered species are protected in Kruger National Park in northeastern South Africa, along the Mozambique border. The park was named after Paul Kruger, leader of the Afrikaners (people of Dutch descent), who fought the British in the Boer Wars in the late 19th century.

0   100 miles
0   100 kilometers

Messina

Limpopo

Pietersburg

KRUGER
NAT.
PARK

Mafikeng

Tshwane (Pretoria)

Middelburg

Johannesburg

Germiston

Soweto

Springs

Klerksdorp

Vereeniging

Kuruman

Vaal

Kroonstad

Welkom

Bethlehem

Ladysmith

Empangeni

Kimberley

Thabana-Ntlenyana
11,424ft (3,482m)

Bloemfontein

Maseru

Pietermaritzburg

A F R I C A

LESOTHO

Durban

Orange

D R A K E N S B E R G   M T S

Umtata

Graaff-Reinet

Queenstown

Grahamstown

East London

Uitenhage

INDIAN OCEAN

Port Elizabeth

PEOPLE AND BELIEFS

Africa is home to almost 14 percent of the world's population. Huge areas are thinly populated, others are overcrowded. Densely populated areas include the Nile valley and northwest coast, parts of West Africa, the lakelands of East Africa and southeastern Africa.

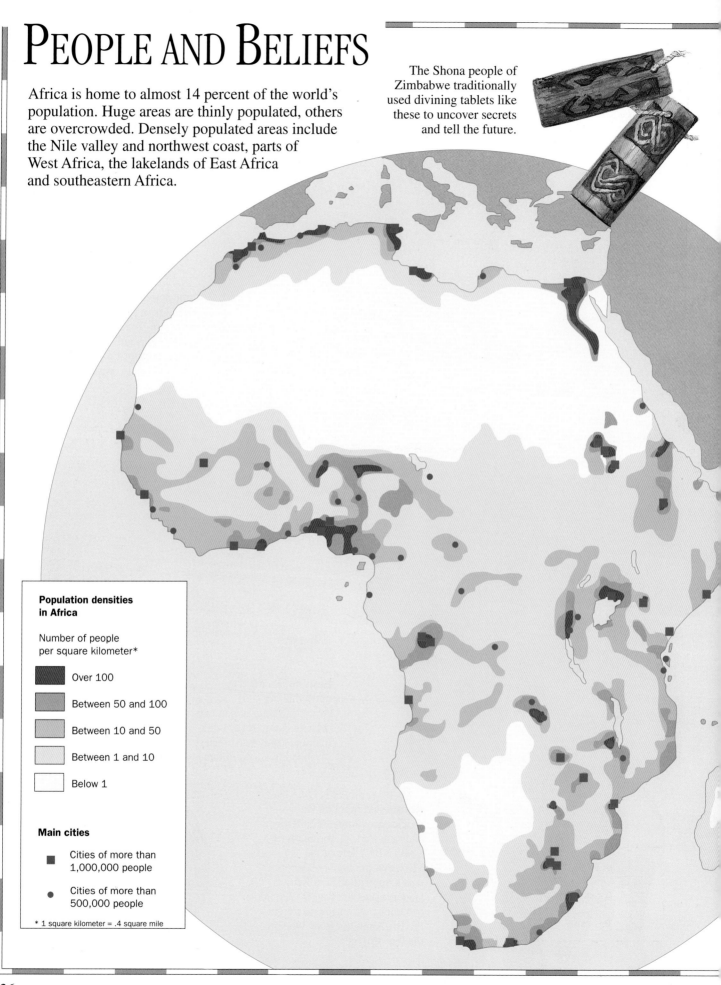

The Shona people of Zimbabwe traditionally used divining tablets like these to uncover secrets and tell the future.

Population densities in Africa

Number of people per square kilometer*

Over 100

Between 50 and 100

Between 10 and 50

Between 1 and 10

Below 1

Main cities

■ Cities of more than 1,000,000 people

● Cities of more than 500,000 people

* 1 square kilometer = .4 square mile

Population and area

Africa's largest countries are Sudan, Algeria and the Democratic Republic of Congo. Sudan contains large, thinly populated deserts, swamps and humid rainforests, while many people are concentrated in the Nile valley. Nigeria, the thirteenth largest country, has the highest population in Africa. But the most crowded countries on the African mainland are Rwanda and Burundi. About one-third of Africa's people live in cities and towns. The largest city is Cairo.

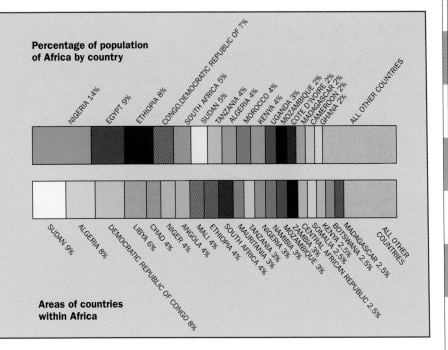

Percentage of population of Africa by country

NIGERIA 14% · EGYPT 9% · ETHIOPIA 8% · CONGO, DEMOCRATIC REPUBLIC OF 7% · SOUTH AFRICA 5% · SUDAN 5% · TANZANIA 4% · ALGERIA 4% · MOROCCO 4% · KENYA 4% · UGANDA 3% · MOZAMBIQUE 2% · COTE D'IVOIRE 2% · MADAGASCAR 2% · CAMEROON 2% · GHANA 2% · ALL OTHER COUNTRIES

SUDAN 9% · ALGERIA 8% · DEMOCRATIC REPUBLIC OF CONGO 8% · LIBYA 6% · CHAD 4% · NIGER 4% · ANGOLA 4% · MALI 4% · ETHIOPIA 4% · SOUTH AFRICA 4% · MAURITANIA 4% · TANZANIA 3% · NIGERIA 3% · NAMIBIA 3% · MOZAMBIQUE 3% · ZAMBIA 3% · CENTRAL AFRICAN REPUBLIC 3% · SOMALIA 2.5% · KENYA 2.5% · BOTSWANA 2.5% · MADAGASCAR 2.5% · ALL OTHER COUNTRIES

Areas of countries within Africa

Main religions

In the seventh century CE, Arabs spread from Arabia across North Africa, converting people to Islam. In the Middle Ages, Islam spread south of the Sahara, especially into West and East Africa. Today, almost 40 percent of Africa's people are Muslims. The Ethiopian Christian Church has existed since the fourth century CE. But Christianity did not reach most of Africa south of the Sahara until the 19th century. Today, about 44 percent of the people of Africa are Christians. Most other Africans follow traditional religions. These religions vary, but all of them contain a belief in one supreme being.

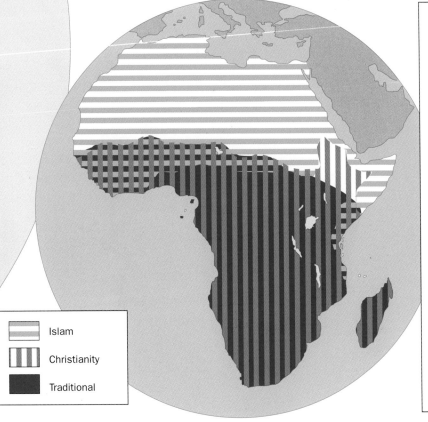

Islam
Christianity
Traditional

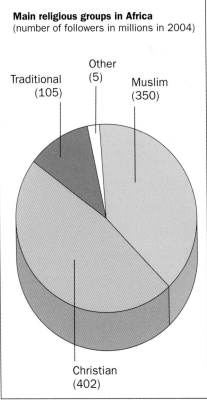

Main religious groups in Africa
(number of followers in millions in 2004)

Traditional (105)
Other (5)
Muslim (350)
Christian (402)

CLIMATE AND VEGETATION

Rainforests grow in the tropical rainy climatic region around the equator. Savanna (grassland with scattered trees) occurs in places with tropical climates with wet and dry seasons. The savanna regions merge into dry grasslands and deserts. Mediterranean climates, with hot, dry summers and mild, rainy winters, occur in the far northwest and southwest.

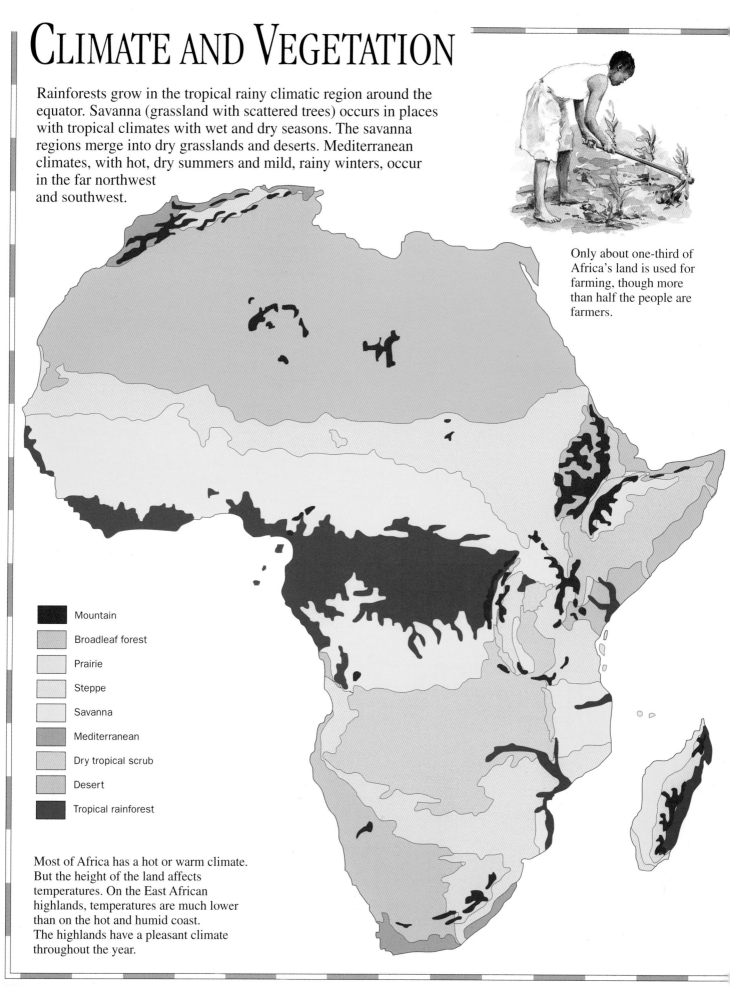

Only about one-third of Africa's land is used for farming, though more than half the people are farmers.

Legend:
- Mountain
- Broadleaf forest
- Prairie
- Steppe
- Savanna
- Mediterranean
- Dry tropical scrub
- Desert
- Tropical rainforest

Most of Africa has a hot or warm climate. But the height of the land affects temperatures. On the East African highlands, temperatures are much lower than on the hot and humid coast. The highlands have a pleasant climate throughout the year.

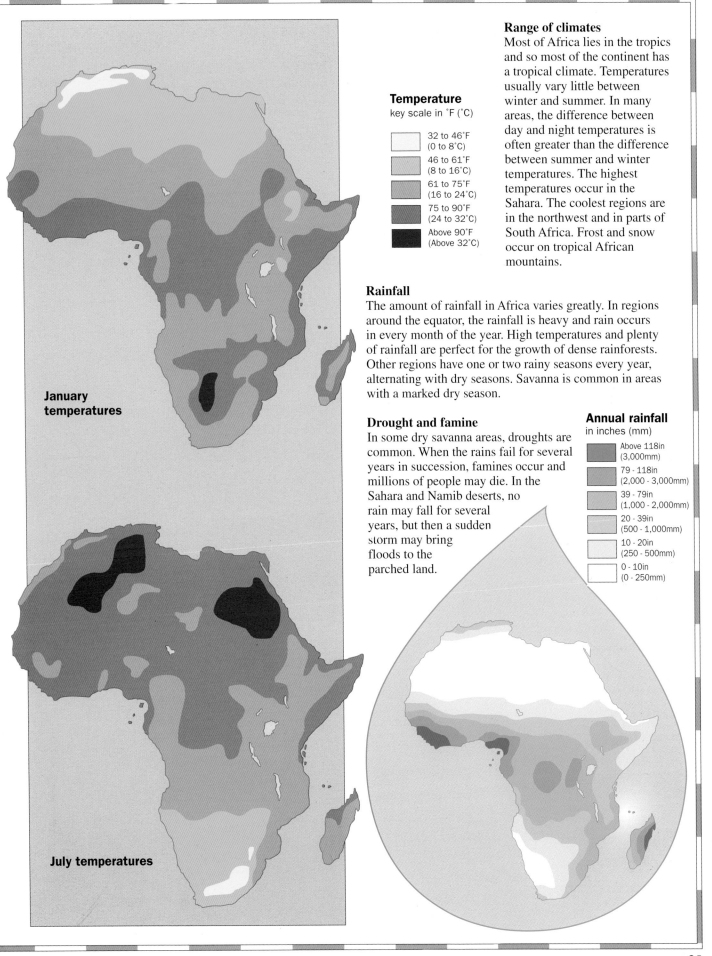

January temperatures

July temperatures

Range of climates

Most of Africa lies in the tropics and so most of the continent has a tropical climate. Temperatures usually vary little between winter and summer. In many areas, the difference between day and night temperatures is often greater than the difference between summer and winter temperatures. The highest temperatures occur in the Sahara. The coolest regions are in the northwest and in parts of South Africa. Frost and snow occur on tropical African mountains.

Rainfall

The amount of rainfall in Africa varies greatly. In regions around the equator, the rainfall is heavy and rain occurs in every month of the year. High temperatures and plenty of rainfall are perfect for the growth of dense rainforests. Other regions have one or two rainy seasons every year, alternating with dry seasons. Savanna is common in areas with a marked dry season.

Drought and famine

In some dry savanna areas, droughts are common. When the rains fail for several years in succession, famines occur and millions of people may die. In the Sahara and Namib deserts, no rain may fall for several years, but then a sudden storm may bring floods to the parched land.

Temperature
key scale in °F (°C)

- 32 to 46°F (0 to 8°C)
- 46 to 61°F (8 to 16°C)
- 61 to 75°F (16 to 24°C)
- 75 to 90°F (24 to 32°C)
- Above 90°F (Above 32°C)

Annual rainfall
in inches (mm)

- Above 118in (3,000mm)
- 79 - 118in (2,000 - 3,000mm)
- 39 - 79in (1,000 - 2,000mm)
- 20 - 39in (500 - 1,000mm)
- 10 - 20in (250 - 500mm)
- 0 - 10in (0 - 250mm)

ECOLOGY AND ENVIRONMENT

In the early 2000s, Africa's population was increasing by about 2.4 percent per year – faster than any other continent. The rapid increase in population in the last 50 years has led to the destruction of forests and savanna, causing great damage to the land in many areas.

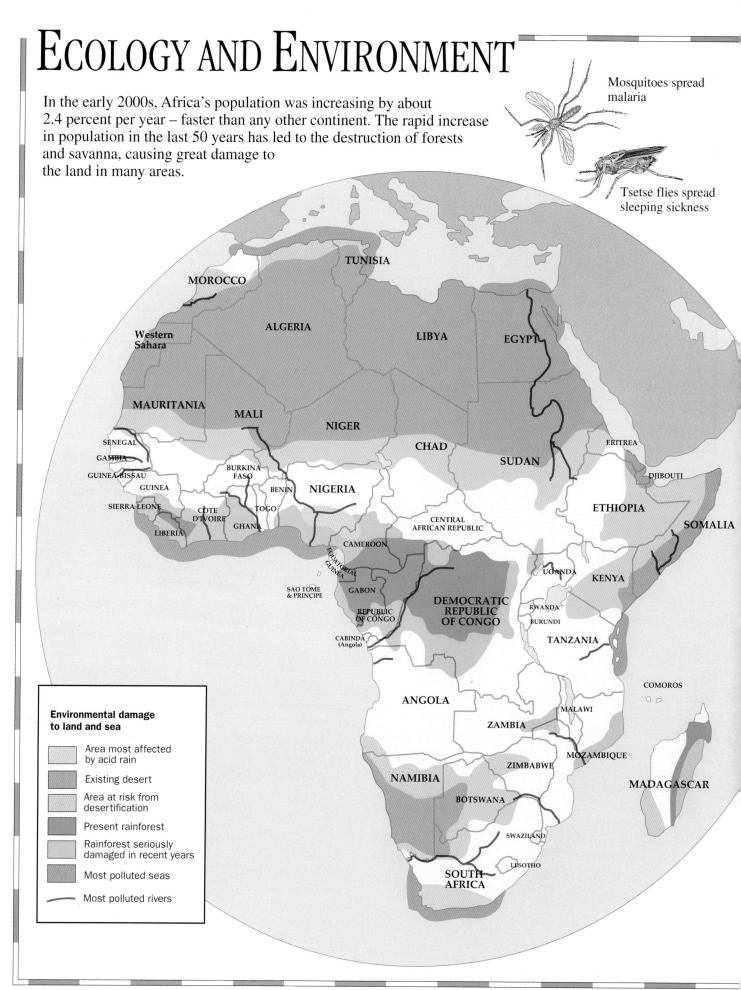

Mosquitoes spread malaria

Tsetse flies spread sleeping sickness

TUNISIA

MOROCCO

Western Sahara

ALGERIA

LIBYA

EGYPT

MAURITANIA

MALI

NIGER

CHAD

SUDAN

ERITREA

SENEGAL

GAMBIA

GUINEA-BISSAU

BURKINA FASO

DJIBOUTI

GUINEA

BENIN

NIGERIA

SIERRA LEONE

CÔTE D'IVOIRE

TOGO

GHANA

LIBERIA

CENTRAL AFRICAN REPUBLIC

ETHIOPIA

SOMALIA

CAMEROON

EQUATORIAL GUINEA

SAO TOME & PRINCIPE

GABON

REPUBLIC OF CONGO

DEMOCRATIC REPUBLIC OF CONGO

UGANDA

KENYA

RWANDA

BURUNDI

TANZANIA

CABINDA (Angola)

COMOROS

ANGOLA

MALAWI

ZAMBIA

MOZAMBIQUE

ZIMBABWE

MADAGASCAR

NAMIBIA

BOTSWANA

SWAZILAND

LESOTHO

SOUTH AFRICA

Environmental damage to land and sea

- Area most affected by acid rain
- Existing desert
- Area at risk from desertification
- Present rainforest
- Rainforest seriously damaged in recent years
- Most polluted seas
- Most polluted rivers

Damaging the environment

The destruction of the natural plant life in any area exposes the soil. When forests are cut down to create farmland, the rain dissolves away plant nutrients in the soil. As a result, exposed soil in tropical rainy areas soon becomes infertile. Farmers then need to add expensive fertilizers to the soil to grow crops.

In dry areas, people graze cattle, sheep and goats. The larger the herds, the greater the destruction of the plants on which the animals feed. The herders also need fuel, so they cut down trees and shrubs. As the numbers of people and animals in dry grassland areas increase, so the rate of plant destruction increases. When the plants are removed, the dry soil is broken up into fine dust. This dust is often blown away by the wind or washed away by storms, leaving bare rock on which nothing can grow. This is called soil erosion.

Natural hazards

Unreliable rainfall and occasional long droughts are major natural hazards in Africa. Droughts lasting several years have occurred in the Sahel. Already scanty vegetation, unable to support an increasing population of people and livestock, has been stripped to bare earth and rock. This process, called desertification, turns once fertile land into desert. The people must migrate or starve. Other hazards include diseases, such as malaria, sleeping sickness and HIV/AIDS. Diseases disable and kill millions of cattle and people.

Natural hazards and diseases

- Earthquake zones
- HIV/AIDS widespread
- Malaria widespread
- Sleeping sickness widespread
- Areas recently affected by famine

Endangered species

Only 50 years ago, the forests and grasslands of Africa supported enormous numbers of wild animals. But the rapid increase in Africa's population has led to widespread destruction of forests and savanna regions once occupied only by animals. Many countries have set up national parks to conserve wildlife. These parks are tourist attractions.

Many animals have been killed for food or for profit. Poachers slaughter elephants for their tusks and all kinds of animals die when people fight wars where they live. They also suffer from exposure to human diseases, such as ebola fever, which caused the deaths of hundreds of gorillas and apes in Central Africa in 2003.

Black rhino

Some endangered species of Africa

Birds
Hermit ibis
Congo peacock
Mauritius kestrel
White-necked picathartes

Mammals
African hunting dog
Aye-aye
Black rhino
Grevy's zebra
Mountain gorilla

Marine animals
Leatherback turtle

Plants
Afrormosia tree
Madagascar periwinkle
Mulanje cedar
Giant protea

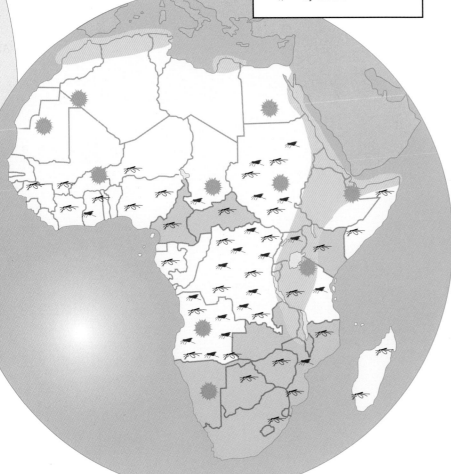

ECONOMY

Africa has many natural resources, including oil and natural gas, and huge deposits of valuable metals and precious stones. Most of the fuels and minerals are exported, however, because Africa lacks the industries to process them. About 60 percent of Africa's people live by farming. Many farmers are poor, producing little more than they need to support their families.

The huge rivers of Africa are capable of producing enormous amounts of electric power.

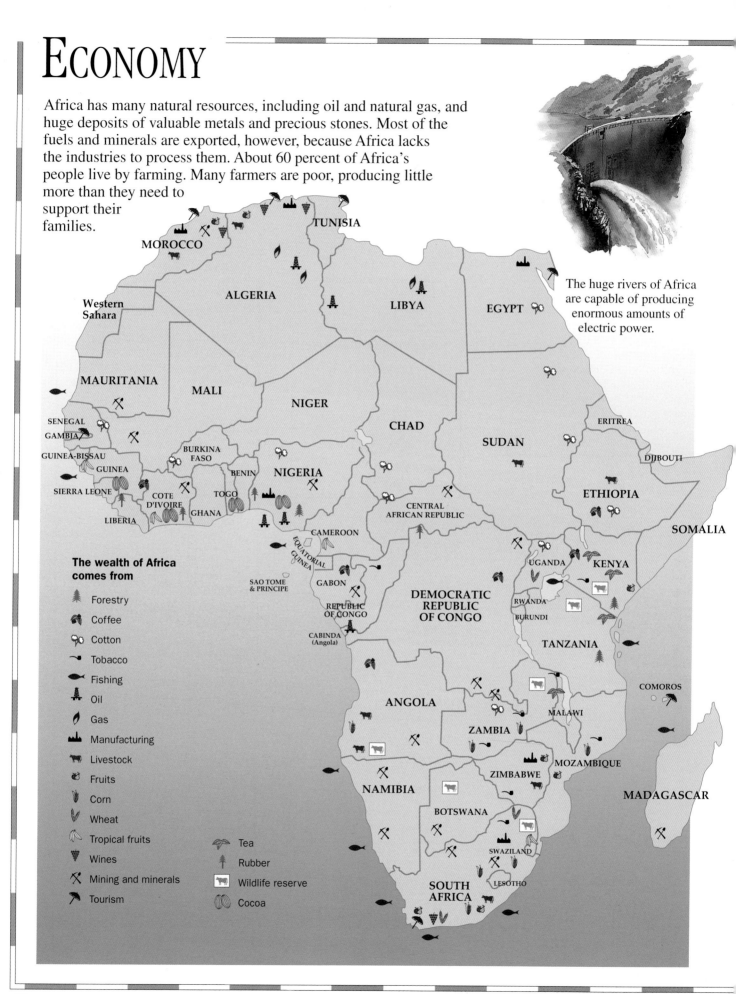

MOROCCO

TUNISIA

ALGERIA

LIBYA

EGYPT

Western Sahara

MAURITANIA

MALI

NIGER

CHAD

SUDAN

ERITREA

DJIBOUTI

SENEGAL
GAMBIA
GUINEA-BISSAU
GUINEA

BURKINA FASO

BENIN

NIGERIA

ETHIOPIA

SIERRA LEONE

COTE D'IVOIRE

TOGO

GHANA

LIBERIA

CENTRAL AFRICAN REPUBLIC

SOMALIA

CAMEROON

EQUATORIAL GUINEA

SAO TOME & PRINCIPE

GABON

REPUBLIC OF CONGO

CABINDA (Angola)

DEMOCRATIC REPUBLIC OF CONGO

UGANDA

KENYA

RWANDA

BURUNDI

TANZANIA

COMOROS

ANGOLA

ZAMBIA

MALAWI

MOZAMBIQUE

ZIMBABWE

MADAGASCAR

NAMIBIA

BOTSWANA

SWAZILAND

SOUTH AFRICA

LESOTHO

The wealth of Africa comes from

- 🌲 Forestry
- Coffee
- Cotton
- Tobacco
- Fishing
- Oil
- Gas
- Manufacturing
- Livestock
- Fruits
- Corn
- Wheat
- Tropical fruits
- Wines
- Mining and minerals
- Tourism
- Tea
- Rubber
- Wildlife reserve
- Cocoa

42

Gross domestic product

In order to compare the economies of countries, experts work out the gross domestic product (GDP) of the countries in US dollars. The GDP is the total value of all the goods and services produced in a country in a year. The chart, right, shows that South Africa's GDP is the highest in Africa. It is more than twice as large as Algeria's, the country with the second highest GDP. South Africa has more industries than any other African country, while Algeria exports gas and oil.

GDP for the countries of Africa (in billions of dollars)

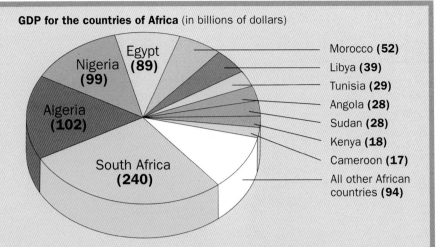

Egypt (89)
Nigeria (99)
Algeria (102)
South Africa (240)
Morocco (52)
Libya (39)
Tunisia (29)
Angola (28)
Sudan (28)
Kenya (18)
Cameroon (17)
All other African countries (94)

Sources of energy

Although Africa mostly lacks coal, several countries produce oil and natural gas. Major exporters include Nigeria, Libya and Algeria. Egypt is another oil producer, but it uses most of its oil. Algeria, Africa's leading producer of natural gas, is one of the world's top ten producers. South Africa is Africa's only major producer of coal.

Hydroelectricity (water power) is important in countries with long rivers. For example, a major hydroelectric plant is located at the High Dam on the River Nile at Aswan, Egypt. The Democratic Republic of Congo, Ghana and Mozambique also have large hydroelectric power projects, while Zambia and Zimbabwe share the Kariba Gorge hydroelectric complex on the Zambezi River.

Per capita GDPs

Per capita means per head or per person. Per capita GDPs are worked out by dividing the GDP by the population. South Africa's per capita GDP is US $5,434, much lower than the United States' per capita GDP of $41,733. But many African countries are poor, with extremely low per capita GDPs. For example, the per capita GDP of Mozambique is only $336.

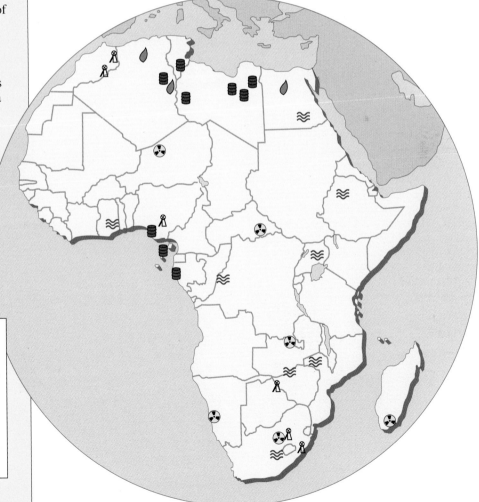

Sources of energy found in Africa

- Oil
- Gas
- Hydroelectricity
- Coal
- Uranium

POLITICS AND HISTORY

Africa contains 53 independent countries. Morocco in North Africa and Lesotho and Swaziland in southern Africa are monarchies. Morocco occupies Western Sahara, but some local people believe that it should be a separate, independent country. Most African countries are republics though many are not fully democratic.

Since achieving independence, the progress of many countries has been slowed by instability. Civil wars and military takeovers have occurred in many countries, with military leaders replacing civilian governments.

Great events

Fossil evidence suggests that the evolution of the human species may have taken place in Africa.

Around 3100 BCE, northeastern Africa was the site of a great early civilization, Ancient Egypt. In the Middle Ages, several major kingdoms, such as Ancient Ghana and Mali, flourished in West Africa. We owe our knowledge of these kingdoms to the Arabs, who traded with them.

European influence south of the Sahara began in the 15th century. At first, Europeans seldom went inland. Instead, they traded for slaves, gold and other valuable goods on the coast. In the late 19th century, most of Africa came under European rule. But from the 1950s, the countries of Africa gradually won their independence. In 1994, South Africa held its first election with all of its citizens being able to vote. Nelson Mandela was elected president.

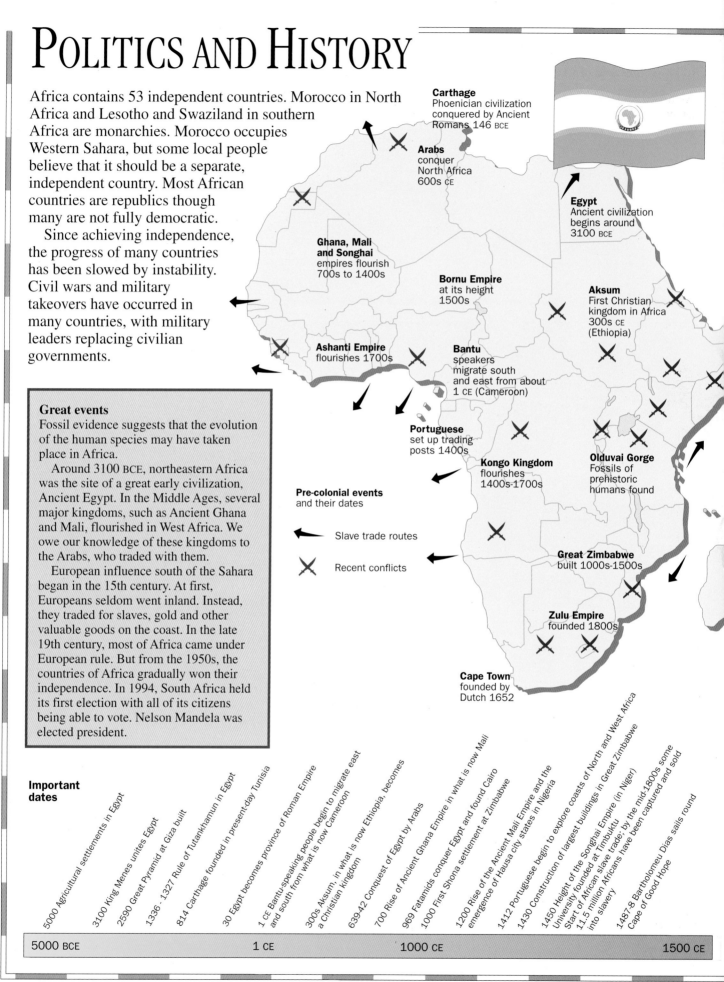

Carthage
Phoenician civilization conquered by Ancient Romans 146 BCE

Arabs conquer North Africa 600s CE

Egypt
Ancient civilization begins around 3100 BCE

Ghana, Mali and Songhai empires flourish 700s to 1400s

Bornu Empire at its height 1500s

Aksum
First Christian kingdom in Africa 300s CE (Ethiopia)

Ashanti Empire flourishes 1700s

Bantu speakers migrate south and east from about 1 CE (Cameroon)

Portuguese set up trading posts 1400s

Kongo Kingdom flourishes 1400s-1700s

Olduvai Gorge
Fossils of prehistoric humans found

Pre-colonial events and their dates

→ Slave trade routes

✕ Recent conflicts

Great Zimbabwe built 1000s-1500s

Zulu Empire founded 1800s

Cape Town founded by Dutch 1652

Important dates

5000 Agricultural settlements in Egypt

3100 King Menes unites Egypt

2590 Great Pyramid at Giza built

1336 - 1327 Rule of Tutankhamun in Egypt

814 Carthage founded in present-day Tunisia

30 Egypt becomes province of Roman Empire

1 CE Bantu-speaking people begin to migrate east and south from what is now Cameroon

300s Aksum, in what is now Ethiopia, becomes a Christian kingdom

639-42 Conquest of Egypt by Arabs

700 Rise of Ancient Ghana Empire in what is now Mali

969 Fatamids conquer Egypt and found Cairo

1000 First Shona settlement at Zimbabwe

1200 Rise of the Ancient Mali Empire and the emergence of Hausa city states in Nigeria

1412 Portuguese begin to explore coasts of North and West Africa

1430 Construction of largest buildings in Great Zimbabwe

1450 Height of the Songhai Empire (in Niger) University founded at Timbuktu

Start of African slave trade; by the mid-1800s some 11.5 million Africans have been captured and sold into slavery

1487-8 Bartholomeu Dias sails round Cape of Good Hope

5000 BCE	1 CE	1000 CE	1500 CE

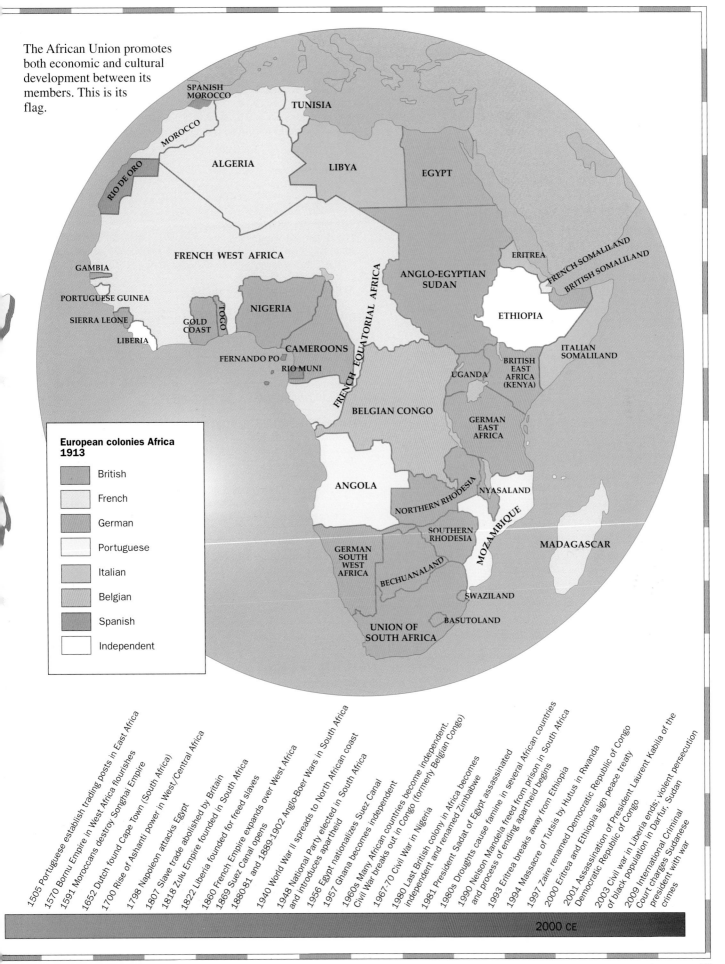

The African Union promotes both economic and cultural development between its members. This is its flag.

European colonies Africa 1913

- British
- French
- German
- Portuguese
- Italian
- Belgian
- Spanish
- Independent

SPANISH MOROCCO

TUNISIA

MOROCCO

RIO DE ORO

ALGERIA

LIBYA

EGYPT

FRENCH WEST AFRICA

GAMBIA

ERITREA

FRENCH SOMALILAND

ANGLO-EGYPTIAN SUDAN

BRITISH SOMALILAND

PORTUGUESE GUINEA

SIERRA LEONE

NIGERIA

GOLD COAST

TOGO

LIBERIA

ETHIOPIA

CAMEROONS

FERNANDO PO

RIO MUNI

ITALIAN SOMALILAND

FRENCH EQUATORIAL AFRICA

UGANDA

BRITISH EAST AFRICA (KENYA)

BELGIAN CONGO

GERMAN EAST AFRICA

ANGOLA

NYASALAND

NORTHERN RHODESIA

MOZAMBIQUE

SOUTHERN RHODESIA

MADAGASCAR

GERMAN SOUTH WEST AFRICA

BECHUANALAND

SWAZILAND

BASUTOLAND

UNION OF SOUTH AFRICA

1505 Portuguese establish trading posts in East Africa

1570 Bornu Empire in West Africa flourishes

1591 Moroccans destroy Songhai Empire

1652 Dutch found Cape Town (South Africa)

1700 Rise of Ashanti power in West/Central Africa

1798 Napoleon attacks Egypt

1807 Slave trade abolished by Britain

1818 Zulu Empire founded in South Africa

1822 Liberia founded for freed slaves

1860 French Empire expands over West Africa

1869 Suez Canal opens

1880-81 and 1889-1902 Anglo-Boer Wars in South Africa

1940 World War II spreads to North African coast

1948 National Party elected in South Africa and introduces apartheid

1956 Egypt nationalizes Suez Canal

1957 Ghana becomes independent

1960s Many African countries become independent

1967-70 Civil War breaks out in Congo (formerly Belgian Congo)

1980 Last British colony in Africa becomes independent and renamed Zimbabwe

1981 President Sadat of Egypt assassinated

1980s Droughts cause famine in several African countries

1990 Nelson Mandela freed from prison in South Africa and process of ending apartheid begins

1993 Eritrea breaks away from Ethiopia

1994 Massacre of Tutsis by Hutus in Rwanda

1997 Zaire renamed Democratic Republic of Congo

2000 Eritrea and Ethiopia sign peace treaty

2001 Assassination of President Laurent Kabila of the Democratic Republic of Congo

2003 Civil war in Liberia ends; violent persecution of black population in Darfur, Sudan

2009 International Criminal Court charges Sudanese president with war crimes

2000 CE

GLOSSARY

abolish To put an end to.

apartheid An official policy formerly practiced in the Republic of South Africa that separated the different non-white peoples living there and gave privileges to those of European descent.

arable Land that is suitable for planting crops.

arrogant Feeling or showing self-importance and contempt or disregard for others.

aye-aye A small primate that lives in trees and has a long bushy tail, long boy fingers, and teeth resembling those of a rodent. It lives in rainforests of Madagascar, and is most active at night.

cash crop A crop that is grown for direct sale, not for personal consumption.

dictator A powerful leader who rules a country with absolute power, usually by force.

divining tablet A tablet used by a diviner, a person thought to have magical power or insight, to foretell the future or reveal secrets.

endangered Exposed to danger or risk of extinction; animal and plant species are considered to be endangered if they are at risk of dying out.

export To send goods for sale or exchange to other countries.

famine Severe shortage of food, resulting in widespread hunger.

import To bring something in from another country, usually for commercial or industrial purposes.

Islam Muslim religion, a monotheistic religion based on the word of God as revealed to Muhammad during the 7th century.

malnutrition A lack of healthy foods in the diet, or overeating unhealthy foods, leading to physical harm.

monarchy A political system in which a state is ruled by a monarch, such as a king or queen, and who usually rules for life.

mosque A building in which Muslims worship.

natural resources A naturally occurring material, such as coal or wood, that can be exploited by people.

nomads People who move seasonally from place to place to search for food and water or pasture for their livestock.

parched Dry; completely lacking in moisture because of hot conditions or lack of rainfall.

poachers People who hunt or fish illegally.

potash A potassium compound, often used in fertilizers.

rebel A soldier who belongs to a force that seeks to overthrow a government or ruling power.

republic A political system or form of government in which people elect representatives to exercise power for them.

savanna A flat grassland, sometimes with scattered trees, in a tropical or subtropical region.

upland Land that has a high elevation or a region that lies in the interior of a country.

FOR MORE INFORMATION

Africa Cultural Center USA
P.O. Box 5771
Hercules, CA 94547
(510) 234-8822
Web site: http://www.africanculturalcenter.org
The center works toward advancing international and intercultural understanding.

British Museum
Great Russell Street
London, England WC1B 3DG
+44 (0)20 7323 8299
Web site: http://www.britishmuseum.org
The British Museum maintains a Web site containing information about Egyptian life, geography, religion, architecture, trades, and writing, www.ancientegypt.co.uk/menu.html.,

National Museum of African Art
Smithsonian Institution
P.O. Box 37012; MRC 708
Washington, DC 20560
(202) 633-4600
Web site: http://africa.si.edu/
The Smithsonian's National Museum of African Art encourages the discovery and appreciation of the visual arts of Africa, "the cradle of humanity."

National Museum of Natural History
Smithsonian Institution
Tenth Street and Constitution Avenue NW
Washington, DC 20560
(202) 633-1000
Web site: http://www.mnh.si.edu/africanvoices
African Voices in a permanent exhibition at the museum, which examines the life, culture, and art of the diverse peoples of Africa.

Natural History Museum of Los Angeles County Foundation
900 Exposition Boulevard
Los Angeles, CA 90007
(213) 763-3466
Web site: http://www.nhm.org/africa/
The museum's Web site offers information about the continent of Africa and its people.

WEB SITES

Due to the changing nature of Internet links, Rosen Publishing has developed an online list of Web sites related to the subject of this book. This site is updated regularly. Please use this link to access the list:

http://www.rosenlinks.com/atl/africa

FOR FURTHER READING

Badejo, Diedre L., ed. *The African Union* (Global Organizations). New York, NY: Chelsea House Publishers, 2008.

Bramwell, Neil D. *Ancient Egypt* (Civilizations of the Ancient World). Berkeley Heights, NJ: Enslow Publishers, Inc., 2004.

Croze, Harvey. *Africa for Kids: Exploring a Vibrant Continent, 19 Activities* (For Kids). Chicago, IL: Chicago Review Press, 2006.

Currie, Stephen. *West Africa* (Exploration and Discovery). Farmington Hills, MI: Lucent, 2004.

DiPiazza, Francesca Davis. *Algeria in Pictures* (Visual Geography Series). Minneapolis, MN: Twenty-First Century Books, 2008.

Jenson-Elliott, Cynthia L. *East Africa* (Indigenous Peoples). Farmington Hills, MI: Lucent, 2002.

Martin, Michael J. *Apartheid in South Africa* (World History). Farmington Hills, MI: Lucent, 2006.

Murray, Jocelyn. *Africa* (Cultural Atlas for Young People). Updated by Brian A. Stewart. 8 vols. New York, NY: Chelsea House Publishers, 2007.

Pelusey, Michael, and Jane Pelusey. *Africa* (Continents). New York, NY: Chelsea House Publishers, 2004.

Seidman, David. *Teens in South Africa* (Global Connections). Compass Point Books, 2008.

Weltig, Matthew S. *The Aftermath of the Anglo-Zulu War* (Aftermath of History). Minneapolis, MN: Twenty-First Century Books, 2009.

Woods, Michael, and Mary B. Woods. *Seven Natural Wonders of Africa* (Seven Wonders). Minneapolis, MN: Twenty-First Century Books, 2009.

Woods, Michael, and Mary B. Woods. *Seven Wonders of Ancient Africa* (Seven Wonders). Minneapolis, MN: Twenty-First Century Books, 2009.

INDEX

ABOUT THE AUTHORS

Rusty Campbell is a writer who lives in White Plains, New York.

Malcolm Porter is a leading cartographer for children's books. He has contributed to the *Times Atlas* and *Reader's Digest Atlas*, and has provided maps for leading educational and trade publishers. He drew the maps and designed the award-winning books *Atlas of the United States of America* and the *Collins Children's Atlas*.

Keith Lye is a best-selling author of geography titles for children of all ages. He is a distinguished contributor and consultant to major encyclopedias, including *Encyclopedia Britannica* and *World Book*.

PICTURE CREDITS
Photographs: AS Publishing 9
The Hutchinson Library 6, 11, 12, 15, 18, 20, 25, 29, 30, 33
Travel Photo International 27, 34